Douglas County High School Library
333.1 PRO

TOP SECRET RESUMES *For The '90s!*

Copyright, © 1993 by Steven Provenzano, President,
ADVANCED Resume Services, Inc. and DeskTop Publishing, Inc.
Offices in Schaumburg and Roselle, IL 60172

ISBN: 0-9633558-1-3   TXU: 501 504

Library of Congress Catalog Card Number: 93-70858

ALL RIGHTS RESERVED

This book may not be reproduced, in whole or in part, by any means electronic or mechanical, including photocopying, recording, or by any information storage and retrieval system, with the exception of short phrases or sentences used in the writing of the reader's own resume, without express, written permission from the author, Steven A. Provenzano, *ADVANCED* Resume Services, Inc. and DeskTop Publishing, Inc., 701 E. Irving Park Road #201, Roselle, IL 60172.
Telephone: 708/582-1089 or 708/517-1088.

**QUANTITY DISCOUNTS
HOW TO ORDER MORE COPIES:**

TOP SECRET RESUMES *For The '90s!* may be ordered by mail or phone. Contact *ADVANCED* Resume Services, Inc. & DeskTop Publishing, Inc. at the above address. VISA/MC/AMEX accepted. You may also call either phone number listed above for further information and quantity discounts.

Dedicated to my family and friends, the finest in the world. Special thanks to Staff Writer Stephan Burdan, *ADVANCED* Resume Services, Inc. and to Cindy Caravello of Desktop Staffing, Inc. for her help in cover design.

TABLE OF CONTENTS

1. **WRITING A RESUME FOR THE '90s** — 1
   - A Word On Resume Style and Philosophy — 3
   - Some Major Myths Debunked — 4
   - Just What Is a "TOP SECRET RESUME"? — 5
   - What You Must Include In Your Resume — 9
   - What You Shouldn't Include In Your Resume — 11
   - Optional Material — 13

2. **GETTING STARTED: THE RAW MATERIALS** — 14
   - It Can Always Be Better
   - Assess Your Talents — 15
   - Organizing The Resume To Suit Your Needs — 16
   - Should I Use An OBJECTIVE? — 17
   - One Page Or Two? — 18
   - Weeding 'Em Out — 18
   - WORK SHEETS — 19
   - Tips For A High-Impact Resume — 25
   - Creating The EMPLOYMENT Section — 25
   - Creating The EXPERIENCE Section — 28

3. **OUTLINES FOR THE MAJOR PROFESSIONS** — 30
   - Sales Representatives, Computer Programmers, Accountants,
   - Executives, Attorneys, Physicians & Secretaries — 31
   - Engineers: Mechanical, Electronic, Chemical — 32
   - College Graduates (New) — 33
   - Housewives/Homemakers — 34
   - VETERANS Returning To The Work Force — 34
   - The OBJECTIVE — 35
   - Boring Phrases VS. Better — 36
   - Power Words — 37

4. **NOTES ON FORMAT** — 38
   - Some Tricks Of The Trade
   - Line Length & Optical Centering — 40-41
   - What Color Paper; Typefaces & Fonts — 42

5. **TOP SECRET RESUME EXAMPLES** — 45
   - Notations for numbered arrows on first 12 resumes — 46-50

   RESUME EXAMPLES — 51-185

(I)

6. COVER LETTERS   186
   General Tips
   Writing The Cover Letter   187

7. EXAMPLES: COVER LETTERS AND FOLLOW-UP LETTERS
     REFERENCE AND SALARY HISTORY SHEETS   191

8. BROADCAST LETTERS   200
   General Format   201
   Broadcast Letter Example   203

9. USING YOUR RESUME EFFECTIVELY   204
   List of Resource Materials   206

10. AT LAST: THE INTERVIEW   209

    RESUME INDEX BY PROFESSION   211

1

WRITING A RESUME FOR THE '90s

Welcome to the resume guide for the '90s. After writing more than 3,000 resumes in my career with leading resume firms and more than a year in corporate recruiting, I've learned the most important fact of job-hunting: the best person doesn't always get the interview. Rather, it's the person who presents him or herself in the most clear, concise and professional manner.

This guide will show you how to write a high-impact self marketing tool that does justice to you and your hard-earned skills. It will help *you* be the person who's chosen for the interview, and hopefully, the job. Whether you're a seasoned executive or straight out of school, there's an average and an excellent way to present yourself on paper. Presenting yourself in the best possible manner can make the difference between getting a job next week or three months from now, or between a starting salary of $40,000 or $44,000.

Some people think writing a resume is simple. They write brief descriptions of their work history and education, have it typeset - or typed and photocopied - and hope for the best. The results are usually not very good. A typical one-inch advertisement in the Sunday paper can draw hundreds of resumes, and research tells us that most of these have only a few seconds to grab the reader's attention and get them to read the entire resume, let alone call you in for a personal interview.

Writing an effective resume may not be simple, but it doesn't have to be drudgery either. Think of writing your resume as a discovery process. Here's your chance to review your knowledge and accomplishments in your chosen field and decide what direction your career should take. It also helps prepare you for interview questions and can actually create new career choices, when you see that your qualifications may be applicable to new positions, or even whole new industries. Resumes are here to stay as a necessary evil in the business world. The resume game is a numbers game, and the only way to win is to out-write the competition.

If you or someone you know have ever had to hire an employee, then you know how tedious it is to wade through seemingly countless resumes. "They all start to look the same," a colleague told me, and he was right. What he really meant was that they all started to *read* the same. Rather than listing only job responsibilities and accomplishments, the examples in this book emphasize *marketing your abilities*.

Of course, mailing out a resume isn't the only way to get an interview. There's personal networking, i.e. friends, former co-workers and clients, and cold-calling target companies. Market studies show that 60-80 percent of professionals get their jobs through informal referrals. About 15 percent are filled through search firms, 10 percent through mass mailings and only about 5 percent through published advertisements! Nor can any resume "get you a job", only you can do that, although it certainly can prevent you from getting one. However, an excellent presentation of your talents can increase your chances of getting an interview, where it then becomes secondary and you get the chance to personally sell your qualifications.

- TIPSTER -

No matter what method you use to "get your foot in the door," the interviewer will most likely use your resume as the main source of information on your background during the meeting. That's why resumes are so important no matter how they're used.

A Word On Resume Style And Philosophy

The resume examples presented in this guide have impact and raw data, but they also have a degree of style and grace, things you must keep in mind when writing your self-marketing tool. Of course, no resume guide can tell you the exact wording that'll work best for you, but these resumes demonstrate techniques I've used successfully for thousands of clients in almost every field. They are the result of direct feedback from my clients and from employers and were refined through trial and error. Feel free to use any of the wording from these samples to develop your own presentation. Names, addresses, company names and position descriptions have been changed or altered in the interest of confidentiality. Every single profession cannot be represented, so I've tried to include a cross-section of the most common positions.

I recommend reading this entire guide before sitting down to write, but you may also skip ahead to the resume examples and use words and phrases that best suit your needs. If you still need help writing about yourself, check your library for resume samples related to your individual profession, if they're not included here. Because so many resume guides offer conflicting advice or outdated formats, look for language related to the job you're seeking and use the formats and writing techniques presented here.

A list of active verbs is included for use in both the EXPERIENCE and EMPLOYMENT sections, discussed later. As for adjectives, be sure to use them sparingly. When managers or personnel representatives come across vast wastelands of gobbledygook, they may just scan every job title you've had and look for one which vaguely matches their needs. If one doesn't catch their eye, then it's on to the next one in the stack, and all that expensive paper and typesetting was for naught. Remember, it is always *content* that matters most. Paper, typeface and format are important, but they run second place to content in the reader's mind.

Some Major Myths Debunked

Before we get started, keep in mind that there's no such thing as a resume that will "get you a job". People get jobs, not resumes. Resumes can help (or prevent) you from getting *interviews*, but it's up to *you* to get the job through research, written & oral correspondence, and effective interviewing. And remember, a resume "format" that works for one person may not work for you. It's all a combination of your individual talents, your industry and the job market at any given time. I've seen customers walk in with poorly written resumes they claim have gotten them interviews. That's because their skills were in demand at a given time and place. However a perfect resume is essential for *the rest of us*, if you will, competing for too few jobs in a tough economy. That is why there's really no "best" resume format or writing technique, only those that seem to work more often than others and tailored for certain situations. And just because a resume "style" or "format" seemed to attract interviews for your brother's friend's wife doesn't mean it'll work for you!

The overall *format* for most samples in this book (usually: EXPERIENCE or SUMMARY or PROFILE, EMPLOYMENT and EDUCATION sections, with bullets), is still in use by many resume companies, the largest of which I worked for before starting my own. Wordings and formats have been greatly refined for this book and this is the cream-of-the-crop, the latest writing techniques.

After Writing Your Resume: Recommended Reading

There's a brief section at the end of this book outlining interview techniques, along with a list of recommended books. For an overall guide to interviewing and job hunting, I recommend Vicki Spina's *Getting Hired In The '90s* published in January 1993. If you can't find it in your local book store, call Corporate Image Publishers at 1-800-247-6553 to order a copy.

Just what is a "TOP SECRET Resume"?

I called this book *TOP SECRET Resumes For The '90s!* because it contains <u>improved and refined</u> writing and format secrets used by many (though certainly not all) "professional resume writers" all over the country. Having worked for some of the nation's largest resume companies, perhaps the most valuable "secret" I could tell you is that unfortunately, some people in the resume business aren't quite as good as they claim to be. The resume business is a strange one. While working for one of the largest resume firms, I saw "writers" coming and going every month or two. Years later, a district manager of this company confessed to me that they finally gave up hiring "writers" all together. They were looking for sales people now. If they could write to some extent, that was fine, but they had to be able to *sell*. I believe it takes at least a year of solid resume writing to become a decent resume writer. However, I've had customers walk in off the street with better resumes than those costing over $200, by writers who've been at it for years. There are many in our business who work under the name "resume service" who have little or no experience in writing, just a computer sitting dormant in their home. Nor are there any "standard rates", except within various companies. In fact, it's everyone for themselves, and from what I've seen, too many people are paying too much for too little.

I really don't want to discourage you from checking out a professional resume service if you have trouble writing your resume after reading this book, or if you're just too busy to deal with the writing and printing chores. Sometimes it just takes another person to sit across from you and ask questions. Just be sure the writer has written at least 1,000 resumes and has one, preferably two years of <u>full-time</u> experience (resume professionals don't do this as a sideline). Avoid paying over $175 for a one page, (cover letter optional) or $300 for a two page resume with at least ten <u>laser prints</u> (not photocopies) on linen or laid paper. Even then, be sure the writing techniques are at least similar to those in this book. Better yet: use this book to write the best resume you can, then go to a professional resume writer and pay only for basic <u>editing</u> and <u>laser printing.</u> This typically runs about one-third the price of full resume writing. Whenever possible, save money on letter/envelope addressing and envelope stuffing by just doing it yourself.

At my resume company, *ADVANCED* Resume Services near Chicago, people get what they pay for, and we charge *less* than companies with a fraction of our experience. Why? Well in a nutshell, we're writers, not salesmen, and I for one don't have the time or energy to try and convince people to pay what many other companies charge. Given the volume of work we do, and the state of the economy, we don't believe it's necessary to gouge the public!

And there's one other thing, you are hereby instructed to:

MAKE A MESS OF THIS BOOK...

This is a manual, a guide, a tool, or what every you need it to be. So make notes in the margins, circle phrases and instructions that apply specifically to your situation. In fact, the more you mess up this book, the more involved you're getting in the writing process and the better you resume will be.

Now on to a better future...

Whenever I write a resume for someone, I put myself in the employer's position and remember the basic tenet which runs through the mind of just about all of them when they pick up your resume:

WHAT CAN YOU DO FOR ME?

This is what employers want to know, and must be told, as soon as they pick up your resume. It is also what employers must comprehend before they will call you in for an interview. It's up to you to answer this simple question in your resume, and the way you answer it tells the reader as much about who you are as what you want from your career.

An employer may wonder: Does this person know how to utilize (or program) the computer systems my company uses? Can he or she use the latest marketing database systems and help increase sales? Can this applicant interpret the federal government's recent changes in statutes regarding environmental issues? Put yourself in the employer's place and these questions get much easier to pose-- and to answer.

What you leave out of your resume is just as important as what you put in. It's okay to break some rules of grammar in the interest of brevity, but limit this to sentences which take "I", "we", "he" or "she" and other pronouns for granted. Omit these words altogether. Use the abbreviated third person voice demonstrated in the EXPERIENCE (summary) sections discussed throughout this book, especially on pages 28 and 29. It is succinct, direct and helps you get straight to your qualifications and *MARKET* them. Also, when space is tight or if you must have all of your qualifications on one page, you can sacrifice or reduce the EXPERIENCE section in favor of applicable work experience.

- TIPSTER -

Although it's always resume *content* that is most important, you should spare no expense in producing a document with the best possible *appearance,* using the guidelines listed in chapter four: NOTES ON FORMAT. A resume is an investment in your future. It is your life, your experience, your career on paper and, when presented correctly, it can quickly pay for itself in the form of more interviews and higher pay.

What You Must Include in Your Resume

For help in jotting down these essentials, be sure to see the worksheets beginning on page 19:

1. **Name, address, phone number.** It's amazing how many people forget to include their phone number on their resume. The reasons for including all this information should be obvious. I've received resumes without phone numbers and needless to say, those applicants didn't get far with our company.

2. **Job Titles.** These can be modified for clarity and to provide an identification which can be understood by as many employers as possible. For instance: Level III Packer/Shipper becomes Shipping Clerk and Junior Assistant Collections Representative becomes Collections Representative.

3. **Company Names.** Unless you've had five or six jobs shorter than one year and are writing a purely functional resume, include company names, the divisions or branches if that helps describe your responsibilities and the towns/cities and states.

4. **Job Responsibilities.** This is the most important part of your resume. Employers must review your previous work history before considering you for themselves. Include part-time employment when the experience gained will apply to the position at hand, but you may also include part-time positions which show initiative or that you "self-funded" a level of college costs, as demonstrated on page 57.

5. **Licenses and Certifications.** Include Insurance and Real Estate sales licenses in addition to other applicable credentials such as C.P.A. Also include Civil Service or Government grades and classifications when appropriate for the type of job you're seeking.

6. **Education.** List the highest level reached first and don't bother listing high school education if you have a college degree. If you're straight out of school with no applicable work

experience, present your education right after your EXPERIENCE (or PROFILE, or SUMMARY of QUALIFICATIONS). Education becomes less important as your hands-on work experience grows. Place it immediately below EMPLOYMENT when you have several years of applicable work history. You may include college attendance and course completions if no degree was earned. Remember to ask yourself: is this applicable to my present career goal? Additional professional training should be included, especially if this was sponsored by an employer; it shows the firm had confidence in your ability to learn and succeed. List which firms sponsored the seminars or college courses.

7. **Languages.** List your level of proficiency: "Speak conversational French," "Fluent in Spanish," "Read and Write Italian", "Familiar with Russian." These can be mentioned in the communications portion of your EXPERIENCE section, or near the bottom in a PERSONAL section as demonstrated in the resumes provided here, including those on pages 53 and 56.

8. **Patents and Publications.** By all means, list articles published in trade journals, magazines, and newspapers, as well as patents on product designs or production techniques.

9. **Professional Groups.** List affiliations or memberships with professional groups. This shows you have an active interest in industry developments and share ideas with fellow professionals. These affiliations can prove very valuable in your job search when you get to personal networking, explained in Chapter 9.

What You Shouldn't Include in Your Resume

In the resume examples which follow, you will see no mention of:

1. **Salary Requirements/History.** If this is requested in the job posting or advertisement, then by all means include it with your resume, but on a separate Salary History sheet and never on the resume itself. If salary information is not requested, then do not offer it; you could be knocked out of consideration for being over or under priced. Concentrate on the interview first and getting an employer interested in you, then you can negotiate compensation.

2. **"Resume" at the top of the page or "References Available Upon Request" at the end.** If your resume cannot be easily identified as such, something needs rewriting. As for references, write three or four names, titles, and phone numbers of previous supervisors, if you are sure they will give you a positive reference. Have these printed or typed on the same quality and color of paper as your resume. Bring this page along with your resume to complete the job application. The personnel representative or hiring manager will almost certainly call your last two or three employers and try to speak directly with your past supervisors if the company is serious about hiring you. Usually someone will check with you before contacting your current employer, but be sure to confirm this at the interview if you are concerned about confidentiality.

3. **Reasons for leaving a job.** If your future employer wants to know why or how you left a job, they can call you and ask. At least then you have them on the line and can begin a rapport. And of course, they can and will ask you at the interview. An EXCEPTION can be made if your last few jobs were unusually short and there are genuinely good reasons for leaving, such as relocation or major company cutbacks due to industry trends. Include a one-

line explanation at the end of your job responsibilities. I suggest this only if you're getting no response from the first 50 resumes mailed.

4. **Religious or political organizations.** Because we all have our prejudices, this type of information often has a better chance of working against you than for you. Always put business considerations first. What do these associations have to do with the position you're seeking? Like anything else, if it won't actually help you get in the door, leave it out. Business fraternities and associations are O.K. to list. EXCEPTION: If you have confusing, little or no job history, but lots of experience with churches, synagogues or social events & groups, (Boy Scouts, Kiwanis, etc.) then you should develop and include this experience on your resume to show communication, organizational and/or leadership skills.

5. **Any negative information.** Your resume is no place to confess your failures or shortcomings. To many employers, resume reading is a process of elimination and you must not give the reader any reason to take you out of the running. Never mention lawsuits, a bad experience with a former supervisor, or any handicap which could seen as affecting your performance on the job.

- TIPSTER -
A resume is all of your positives and none of your negatives. Employers know this as well as you do, and the best ones know how to read between the lines. When they do, there must always be truth and substance to your writing. Omit things if you must/can, but NEVER LIE ON YOUR RESUME. Someday, the lie(s) may catch up with you.

Optional Material

1. **Military Service.** You may include positive military service, especially if seeking a position with a firm involved in defense contracting which hires former military personnel. Include highest rank attained, supervisory experience and applicable training. For technical positions, include systems and equipment operated, repaired or maintained. If your only applicable work experience was in the military, then of course this must be developed like any other job. In this case, I recommend labeling the section EMPLOYMENT rather than MILITARY.

2. **Personal Section.** If it won't push you into a second or third page, include two to three lines outlining your interests in sports and/or exercise. Golf and racquet sports are great for executives. List team sports such as college or park district basketball or baseball. Adding "avid reader and chess player" demonstrates reading and analytical skills and is recommended. Of course, omit items that have no connection to your ability to tackle the job, such as "enjoy basket weaving, crocheting and cooking."

3. **Age and Marital Status.** Legally, these two items should have no bearing on whether you're considered for a position, but they often do in the real world. Listing your age (birthday) can label you as too young or too old no matter what your age. Leave it out all together. Omit marital status, unless you firmly believe this will demonstrate a certain stability and improve your chances of getting an interview for positions such as marriage counselor, or as part of a husband/wife franchise team.

2

GETTING STARTED: THE RAW MATERIALS

It Can Always Be Better

No matter who you are or how great you can write, a *truly* professional writer can probably improve your resume. I've done resumes for some great technical writers who were amazed at the results. That's because I made resumes my specialty. If I needed documentation on integrated circuit design or computer programs, I'd hire a technical writer. If I needed someone to run a company, I'd hire the best executive I could find. Professional writers can write better about you simply because they're NOT you. The best ones can take an objective look at your background, ask you numerous, in-depth questions and create something that has a better chance of impressing an employer and increasing your chances of getting a personal interview.

You must now become your own professional writer. Because I can't sit across from you and ask questions about your experience and education, you must do it yourself. This requires honesty and objectivity. Are you really proficient at *everything* you do? Of course not. On the other hand, don't take any of your applicable experience for granted. It can be fatal to assume an employer already knows what you can do simply because they are already in that particular business.

Assess Your Talents

Before you can write anything about your background, you need to start answering every employer's question: "What Can You Do For Me?"

Get a paper and pencil and draw a line lengthwise down the center. Title one side Knowledge/Talents, and the other side Achievements. To write this page you must stand back and take a long look at your total career background related to the position you're seeking. (For new college graduates, this means getting an idea of how the things you've learned relate to the position you're seeking).

Knowledge/Talents are your marketable abilities and skills, <u>whether or not you've used them on the job.</u> These are the nuts and bolts for your EXPERIENCE section as described on page 28. The Achievements listing should represent a general, overall summary of your achievements for previous employers such as the ability to meet or exceed sales quotas (by what percent?), success in developing new product designs or business systems, and so on.

Imagine yourself already in the position. Think about how your qualifications can be shaped into phrases a job incumbent would appreciate. If you're not sure exactly what field interests you, don't worry. Check the examples in Chapter 5 and just start writing. It's helpful to write down everything you think of first, then narrow it down and make a short list of those items you feel are most applicable to the desired position.

Notice we're really talking about overall **ability** here, not just work history or education, and there is a difference. A college graduate may have many abilities and very little work history. The best way that person can get their first "real" job is to market all of his or her ability. Think of the *type* of work you've done for college projects, charitable organizations or special groups: "report preparation and analysis; data compilation and review; plan and conduct written and oral presentations in a professional manner," etc. This, combined with your education and knowledge of the field, will all help project you as a viable candidate for the position.

Organizing The Resume To Suit Your Needs

Depending on who you talk with about your resume and which books you read on the subject, there are countless ways to write and layout your resume. This guide emphasizes three of the best formats, which can be modified to suit your particular qualifications and career goals:

1. **Chronological or Reverse Chronological.** In this book we call the *chronological* format the one where you put your most recent position first (on top). Physicians, attorneys and most senior-level executives with solid work experience should use this rather conservative approach. As you will see in the resume examples, the EMPLOYMENT section must concisely emphasize your most important duties with a company, skills used which *apply* to your career goals, awards or achievements, and specific benefits you brought to the company. If your most related experience was long ago, don't be afraid to place that at the top, (reverse chronological) following, in order, with the months and years at other positions, and ending with your present job. Dates should be tucked away in the right hand margin. If there are gaps of several months between companies, try using only years. Again, if your current/most recent experience is also the most relevant to your goals, it belongs right on top of the EMPLOYMENT section.

2. **Functional.** This format is best for emphasizing talents and experience most applicable to the position you're seeking, *regardless of employment background.* I highly recommend it if there are major gaps in your work history, or between jobs related to your current OBJECTIVE. It's also recommended for recent college graduates, homemakers or veterans returning to the work force, those with unsuccessful self-employment experience or anyone else with confusing or little work experience.

3. **Combination Chronological/Functional.** This is the format which typically works best for my clients. Here you can market all the best points of your experience and abilities in the EXPERIENCE section, and then back-it-up with your work history. If you omit an OBJECTIVE, the EXPERIENCE section can give the reader a good idea of the type of position for which you're best suited. The first paragraph of the EXPERIENCE section summarizes your years of experience. If it's less than one year, it demonstrates that you have developed useful professional talents that can be of value to the business goals of the target firm.

Remember that none of these concepts are written in stone. The whole idea is to project yourself as *the* person who can tackle the position you're seeking. Typically, the best place to make this projection is in a short EXPERIENCE section (p.28) which creates an air of knowledgeability and respectability. Present yourself as a discriminating professional and you have a much better chance of being perceived as such.

Now to answer the two questions most frequently asked by those trying to write a resume:

Should I Use An Objective?

The debate on this question continues. My writers and I believe you should certainly have some idea about what kind of position you're seeking, even if all you know is that you have great analytical skills and want to be challenged when using them on the job. Having an OBJECTIVE is highly recommended for those who know exactly what position they want. It shows self-assurance, confidence and stability. HOWEVER: if you think summarizing your career goals in one or two sentences is just too narrowing or constricting, then leave it out all together. This is what Vicki Spina suggests in her *Getting Hired In The '90s*. "There may be other positions available for which they may call you," she says. You can still focus the reader and communicate a strong sense of self-direction in the EXPERIENCE section. Think of the bullet points here as a strong nudge to the reader. The first bullet gives him or her a full overview of your most marketable skills, which in turn gives them an idea of what kind of work you're looking for. It's a great way to catch their interest and get them involved in, and focused on, your abilities.

One Page Or Two?

Contrary to popular belief, one page is not always best. Simplicity and impact must work together here. If your career genuinely requires two or even three pages to be fairly and accurately presented, then use two or three pages. Unless you have a variety of applicable work experience or a detailed technical background of more than five years, one page will probably suffice. What's best is what works for you. If you write a concise resume that doesn't fit on one page, don't force it to by omitting important facts. Remember, show mercy on the reader by avoiding the irrelevant: long descriptions of inapplicable jobs or volunteer work, marital status, age, race, etc. The employer who is concerned about any but the first two of these, jobs and volunteer work, is probably breaking the law. Would you work for such a company?

Weeding 'Em Out

As noted earlier, research shows that the average advertisement has only a few seconds to catch the reader's interest. For the same reason, brevity, accuracy and overall appearance are key to a successful resume. If you're not sure how to spell a word, look it up. If you don't know how to type accurately, hire a professional typist or printer. Nothing turns off an employer more than basic spelling or grammar mistakes on a resume. The subconscious impression is: "If this person can't even produce a decent resume, how could he/she possibly handle this job?" Use good margins (3/4 to 1 inch on all sides) and plenty of white space throughout the page. It's more attractive, adds readability and reduces reader fatigue.

WORK SHEETS

NAME:

First _____ Middle _____ Last _____

Address:

Street _____ City _____ State _____ Zip _____

Telephone: Area Code _____ / _____

POSITION / INDUSTRY DESIRED: _____

EMPLOYMENT HISTORY Most recent position first:

From   Company _____

_____ 19___ City / State _____

To   Type of Business _____

_____ 19___ Co. Product / Service _____

             Positions / Titles _____

Responsibilities / Duties _____

_____

Supervisory Duties _____

_____

Accomplishments / Major Achievements / Awards _____

_____

_____

_____

From   Company _____

_____ 19___   City / State _____

To   Type of Business _____

_____ 19___   Co. Product / Service _____

                 Positions / Titles _____

Responsibilities / Duties _____

_____

Supervisory Duties _____

_____

Accomplishments / Major Achievements / Awards _____

_____

_____

_____

From   Company _____

_____ 19___   City / State _____

To   Type of Business _____

_____ 19___   Co. Product / Service _____

                 Positions / Titles _____

Responsibilities / Duties _____

_____

Supervisory Duties _____

_____

Accomplishments / Major Achievements / Awards _____

_____

From   Company _____

_____ 19___   City / State _____

To   Type of Business _____

_____ 19___   Co. Product / Service _____

                 Positions / Titles _____

Responsibilities / Duties _____

_____

Supervisory Duties _____

_____

Accomplishments / Major Achievements / Awards _____

_____

_____

_____

EDUCATIONAL HISTORY Most recent first:

University _____ City / State _____

Degree _____ Year(s) Attended / Graduated: _____

Major _____ Minor _____ GPA (B or higher) _____

Course work / Studies _____

_____

Awards / Scholarships _____

_____

Seminars and Special Training _____

_____

Vocational / Trade School _____ City / State _____

Certificate _____ Dates Attended _____

Special Jobs / Equipment _____

_____

High School _____ Dates Attended _____

MILITARY SERVICE: _____ Dates Enlisted _____

Honorable Discharge? _____ Rank _____

PROFESSIONAL MEMBERSHIPS:

Organization _____ Dates _____

Offices Held _____

Duties / Responsibilities _____

Skills Acquired _____

_____

Organization _____ Dates _____

Offices Held _____

Duties / Responsibilities _____

Skills Acquired _____

_____

Organization _____ Dates _____

Offices Held _____

Duties / Responsibilities _____

Skills Acquired _____

_____

COMMUNITY SERVICES & VOLUNTEER ACTIVITIES:

Organization _____ Offices / Titles Held _____

City / State _____ Dates _____

Specific activities in which you were involved and skills utilized

_____

_____

_____

Organization _____ Offices / Titles Held _____

City / State _____ Dates _____

Specific activities in which you were involved and skills utilized

_____

_____

_____

PERSONAL INTERESTS, SPORTS & HOBBIES:

_____

_____

_____

REFERENCES:

Business:

Name _____ His / Her Job Title _____

Company Name _____ City / State _____

Telephone, Office _____ / _____ Home, if permitted _____ / _____

Name _____ His / Her Job Title _____

Company Name _____ City / State _____

Telephone, Office _____ / _____ Home, if permitted _____ / _____

Name _____ His / Her Job Title _____

Company Name _____ City / State _____

Telephone, Office _____ / _____ Home, if permitted _____ / _____

Personal:

Name _____ His / Her profession _____

Telephone, Office _____ / _____ Home, if permitted _____ / _____

Name _____ His / Her profession _____

Telephone, Office _____ / _____ Home, if permitted _____ / _____

Name _____ His / Her profession _____

Telephone, Office _____ / _____ Home, if permitted _____ / _____

ADDITIONAL NOTES:

_____

_____

_____

Tips For A High-Impact Resume

You must tell the employer the most pertinent details of your duties and accomplishments for previous employers. Sound obvious? Notice that this is different from listing your job description, what someone in the position usually does, or what you were "supposed" to have done in your position. <u>Tell the reader what you accomplished, improved upon, created, developed or sold, and if you excelled, to what degree compared to others in the field or company:</u> "Ranked #1 in sales of ten employees", etc.

Creating the EMPLOYMENT Section

Using the worksheets you've just completed and scanning the resume examples beginning on page 51, get a fresh sheet of paper and begin writing the text for your EMPLOYMENT section. If you decide on a Combination or Functional format, you will need this information to create the EXPERIENCE section. Start with your most recent position and list:

1. Company name.
2. Company location, city and state only.
3. Your job title with the firm. Remember to keep this generic enough so as to be understood by managers at other firms. Keep it simple: Staff Accountant, Senior Chemical Engineer, Warehouseman, etc.
4. Dates at each position, months and years only. If you have gaps of more than three months between jobs, try using only years: 1976-1977; 1977-1982, and so on. Use whichever works best for you, but this must be kept consistent for all positions. List major responsibilities at each position and omit the trivial. To do this, you must think of what you do/did every day which helped contribute to bottom-line profitability or efficiency for the firm. See the

following pages for a breakdown of responsibilities in some of the more common positions and apply these ideas to your background.

5. Now list your most important accomplishments with each company, such as exceeding sales quotas, reducing overhead, speeding response to customers, reducing mistakes in filing and order processing, and so on. If positive, how did you rank among others in your company? Did you help streamline production activities? If this resulted in increased revenues, by how much over what period of time? See *Outlines For The Major Professions* on page 30 for further explanations. Talking out loud about your duties and achievements will help you think, and can make your writing much more understandable. <u>Offset these items below your primary duties with dashes, asterisks or small bullets, as in the following resume examples.</u>

You should be able to do this without misrepresenting yourself and without using fluff or useless verbiage. If you can't, then maybe you're not right for the position, or it's not right for you. It's time to reassess. Are your talents transferable to other fields or markets? Someone who is strong in speech communications or English might be great in sales, and a large number of firms are willing to train newcomers in product applications, client needs assessment and sales presentations.

On the other hand, a sales representative who is used to communicating with a wide range of business people may be great in personnel as a recruiter. Teachers can become trainers; accountants can get into personal investment planning; secretaries can branch off into customer service or billing, and so on.

It's all a matter of how you present your talents related to the position at hand. A great resume must always:

1. Quickly provide facts and/or data about your talents related to the position. This may be included in the OBJECTIVE, EXPERIENCE, or EMPLOYMENT sections. Some resumes will have all three of these elements, while others read better without the first two.

2. Build upon and support itself line after line. This creates an impression of organization, intelligence and increasing responsibility.

3. Create an overall feeling that the person on the resume knows his or her profession extremely well, if such is the case, and can utilize their talents in the employer's business market and/or environment. This is best accomplished in the EXPERIENCE section by combining years of work experience (or training and education) in various aspects of the profession with the jargon of the trade. The EXPERIENCE and EMPLOYMENT sections are the most important parts of your resume, and when developing them, it is essential to keep in mind the discriminating *employer's* point of view. Think about the employer's needs, and write to suit those needs.

- TIPSTER -

Here are some great phrase/sentence starters & qualifiers to market your abilities in the **EXPERIENCE** section:

Proven abilities in... More than (x) years in... Proficient in... Skilled in... Experience in...
Perform... Extensive background in... (or qualifications in...)
Plan and conduct... Compile and present... Hire, train and supervise...
Familiar with... Trained in... Education in... Knowledge of... Assist in...

Creating the EXPERIENCE Section

The EXPERIENCE section is where all your best--and most currently marketable skills are grouped together and *sold* to the reader. Use the information you have in front of you from your Knowledge/Talents and Achievements sheet and the EMPLOYMENT section.

Groupings

Accounting activities can be grouped with cost-effective purchasing, along with all hardware and software brands and types used in the execution of your accounting (or secretarial, or customer service, etc.) duties.

"People" skills should be presented together: staff hiring, training and supervision; group orientation; seminar planning and conducting; performance review and worker motivation; benefits administration and vacation scheduling; and of course management--of how many employees at what level of experience and during what type of projects, operations and/or activities. Did worker output improve under your management? If so, by how much and how quickly? Did your leadership help reduce turnover? By what percent over what length of time? It's great to provide numbers to detail your success, but be sure to avoid making your resume a laundry list or heavy data sheet.

Sales-related activities go great together: account prospecting, acquisition and management; personally developed a Midwestern territory through cold calling and personalized account management; utilize demographic and direct mail sources in new market penetration; plan and conduct sales presentations in a professional manner; effectively train new sales representatives in product applications and assessing client's specific business needs. Emphasize product lines you wish to be associated with and avoid those you would rather stay away from. Mention computer software and equipment used in account tracking, lead follow-up and management. See the samples on the following page. The first set is expanded to six bullet points, but try to keep this at a maximum of three bullets for a one page resume, and five bullets for a two page resume:

EXPERIENCE:
- More than 12 years in virtually all aspects of project engineering, machine design/building and secondary tooling, including full management responsibilities.

- Skilled in equipment design & fabrication from concept to completion; experience with Pneumatic & Hydraulic systems & components, automation equipment, Mechanical & Electrical systems and a full range of custom and specialty products.

- Handle cost-effective purchasing of parts and materials; skilled in vendor relations; handle price quoting, sales presentations and proposal writing.

- Plan and implement budgets; perform job/labor estimates; oversee quality control and hire, train & supervise shop staff and management.

- Proficient in EASY CAD and CAD KEY; familiar with AutoCad and Lotus 1-2-3; skilled machinist, tool & die maker and welder: MIG and Arc.

A possible EXPERIENCE section for a housewife returning, or just entering, the work force:

EXPERIENCE:
- **Bookkeeping and Filing:** Accurately balance monthly bank statements against checkbook entries for an active family of six; maintain all records related to income and real estate taxes.

- **Office Equipment:** Accurate typist (50 wpm); utilize IBM Selectric typewriters and 10-key calculators; experience with photocopy machines.

- **Purchasing:** Handle comparative shopping and cost-effective buying of clothing, food and appliances.

Notice that it's acceptable to use the word EXPERIENCE before this section. Even though it is not employment experience acquired from a paying job, it is most certainly experience acquired through diligence, work, trial & error and intellect. The resume is your chance to translate all of these skills into job-related *abilities*. If you don't like word EXPERIENCE here, use PROFILE or SUMMARY.

3

OUTLINES FOR THE MAJOR PROFESSIONS

Here's a breakdown of points to include for various professions, followed by some tips for college graduates and those without much work experience. These ideas apply to almost all professions; be sure to check the resume samples before writing.

Sales Representatives

Of course meeting or exceeding quotas is an essential element in the sales rep's resume. However you must put this in perspective for the reader. How many other reps also made quota? In your office, your division, your state? Did you meet or exceed quota monthly, annually, or quarterly? Did you receive any special performance awards? If so, explain exactly why you received them: "Earned Golden Pyramid Award for exceeding quota 12 consecutive months." Did you ever train or orient new sales staff in territorial management, client relations or product demonstrations?

The EXPERIENCE section is a great place to reinforce the importance of the best sales talents: "account prospecting, acquisition and management." "Determine and meet specific client needs." "plan and conduct written & oral presentations using audiovisual materials," and so on. Group your best experience in a general manner in the EXPERIENCE section, then back it up with actual hands-on work experience and accomplishments.

Computer Programmers

Be as specific as possible. Mention all of your hardware, software and programming languages in the EXPERIENCE section, and you won't have to repeat yourself quite so much in your EMPLOYMENT section. The best way is to mention all computer-related knowledge but use qualifiers for levels of expertise. For instance "proficient in/with" for software and hardware; "fluent in" for languages; and "familiar with" for anything about which you have only a cursory knowledge. Under EMPLOYMENT you mention projects, applications, and accomplishments *specific to that position.*

Accountants

Do you, or can you handle, manage, supervise, process or maintain payroll, general ledgers, inventories, accounts payable, accounts receivable, billing, etc? If so, on what type of computer and with what type of software? Have you ever, or are you able to, compile and present monthly, quarterly or annual reports (written, orally or both)? Did you assist in the conversion from a manual to a computerized system? It's important to present yourself as more than another number cruncher, so talk about participation in company or community events. Interests in sporting events and hobbies should be placed near the bottom in a PERSONAL section only if these activities don't appear so extensive as to detract from your work performance, and only if this won't take you into a second page.

Senior-Level Executives, Attorneys and Physicians

Here is where the EXPERIENCE section should be kept extremely short, if not omitted completely. Trying to summarize briefly what these positions are about at the top of a resume is usually futile if not impossible. If anything, include a one or two-bullet summary of how many years in the business and your general areas of expertise, then follow with work experience/accomplishments.

Secretaries

The gutsy soldier of the working world and perhaps the most underpaid. The finest secretaries have only two major problems: giving themselves credit for, and writing about the huge variety of what they do every day. First, think of all the correspondence you write, type, collate, file, stamp, mail or FED-EX. Do you write about legal matters, meetings, new office procedures, sales results or special company events? What kind of equipment are you proficient or familiar with -- mailing & stamping machines, personal computers or word processors (list hardware and software), brands and sizes of switchboards? How fast can you type and can you transcribe from dictaphone? Are you good with a 10-key calculator? Have you ever arranged travel itineraries or helped out in billing, customer service or other departments when they were too swamped? Of course, note your professional communication skills via telephone and in-person, as well as any commendations received from clients or management.

Engineers: Mechanical, Electronic, and Chemical

Expand upon projects and type of work you would like to see more of, and downplay those you disliked. Of course mention applicable hardware, software, and language proficiency. Note product applications and don't be afraid to get technical in your wording. Personnel staff may be omitted from the screening process for high-tech jobs, so write at a level your boss would appreciate. Provide details on projects supervised or improved upon, cost analyses, vendor sourcing, technical report writing, interfacing with internal/external technical personnel and presentations to clients.

Every single profession cannot be presented here. But many of these ideas are applicable to all types of jobs. If you lack traditional work experience, concentrate on skills acquired through education. Lacking education, you can emphasize talents and abilities acquired through volunteer work or other daily activities, such as basic home bookkeeping. You can present these in a business-like format, as discussed in the Housewives / Homemakers section on the next page.

New College Graduates

Here you can use the qualifiers "education in" or "training in" to show you have acquired a certain level of knowledge on a given topic. Mention the subjects and lengths of term papers related to the profession: "conducted comprehensive interviews with engineers at the Byron nuclear power plant and wrote a 23-page report outlining safety procedures and apparatus for the prevention of meltdowns," "trained and supervised student volunteers for campus recycling program and increased tonnage of recycled newspapers by 25 percent," "directly involved in [or responsible for] proofreading and editing copy for the 1990 edition of the Campus Profiles yearbook." Mention your GPA only if it's within one point of a straight-A average: 3.0/4.0 or 4.0/5.0, and be sure to mention whether that applies to your major or your overall GPA. Don't make the reader guess! Also list any other campus activities, as long as they don't involve political groups, religious groups, or other affiliations which may draw the wrath of prejudice. Exceptions include fund-raisers involving promotions or other business-like activities where you feel your organizational, communication or leadership talents are worth mentioning, despite the church or political group for which they were performed. As always, market your achievements and abilities, then emphasize or downplay their context as needed.

Listing relevant course titles is recommended, but it's even more important to include what was actually learned and accomplished. Did you attend extra-curricular seminars, speeches or lectures? Conducted by whom and from what profession? Were you a member of campus business, computer or literature clubs? What was your input and how was this membership valuable? Think about everything you learned in those four years and how it can best be utilized in the everyday working world, because that is where you will be called upon to communicate, analyze, react, think, organize and manage.

Marketing your acquired knowledge and abilities as a new college graduate in this manner will distance your resume from the typical data sheet format sent out annually by the millions. See Ed Vogts' example on page 57.

Housewives / Homemakers

For all practical purposes, there are no more housewives of the June Cleaver type. Today's homemaker juggles her/his time between functions better phrased as: chauffeuring, budget planning, cost-effective purchasing, child training and supervising, counseling, meal production and household maintenance services. Remember the EXPERIENCE section example on page 29.

Remember that it's all in the presentation. Here's where a Functional format may work best. Unless you have a specific job objective in mind, simply generalize about the type of position sought and be specific about your abilities.

Veterans Returning to the Work Force

Veterans need to do more with their resume than list their "name, rank and serial number". More than anyone else, they need to market their abilities apart from their actual assignments. I strongly recommend either a functional or combination format with an EXPERIENCE section outlining technical, human resource or clerical skills in general terms: "plan and conduct written and oral presentations; handle system troubleshooting and repair to component level; proven ability to determine and meet goals through personalized staff training and supervision; update and maintain inventories, financial records and schedules" etc. This section is then backed-up with specific on-the-job duties performed on assignment. Review the EXPERIENCE sections presented throughout the resume examples in Chapter 5.

The OBJECTIVE

As previously noted, use an OBJECTIVE whenever possible, but don't worry about leaving it off if it's just too limiting. Here are some examples of statements for your OBJECTIVE. This first one is intentionally general, and applicable for any non-specific position:

> **OBJECTIVE:** A position where planning, organizational, and communication skills would be utilized.

You can be more specific if you have a number of years of "experience", especially if you have no room to list the number of years in an EXPERIENCE section:

> **OBJECTIVE:** A position utilizing 12 years in household budget planning, record keeping, prioritizing and the training/supervision of minors.

Mentioning "training and supervision of minors" might just give the reader a smile, and the motivation to read on. The best OBJECTIVES are specific with a job title & focus whenever possible:

> **OBJECTIVE: Sales Representative**
> A position where profit-building skills would be utilized.

> **OBJECTIVE:** A Secretarial position where proven abilities in record keeping, typing, filing and client relations would be of value.

Don't worry about misleading anyone with your OBJECTIVE. It's used as an introduction to your resume, and you then qualify and quantify the statement in the EXPERIENCE and/or EMPLOYMENT sections. Avoid using the burned-out word "challenging...." it's just not necessary and, well, burned-out.

Here are examples of boring phrases turned into exciting statements for both EXPERIENCE and EMPLOYMENT sections. Break down your duties and highlight the key elements. Notice that it's alright to combine sentences in the same paragraph with a semicolon, as in the fourth BETTER sample below.

BORING

EXPERIENCE Section:

Review profit/loss statements and handle a variety of general accounting duties on a daily basis.

Handle updating of account prospect cards and provide full support to sales personnel.

Purchase equipment directly from manufacturers and utilize a computer to create support materials.

Develop sales ideas and related hardware & software with programmers and technical personnel.

EMPLOYMENT Section:

Supervise 12 Sales Representatives covering a large Midwestern territory.

Wrote an employee procedures manual covering a variety of important topics.

Responsible for daily client contact and sales staff training/supervision.

Operated cash register and sold general drug store merchandise.

BETTER

Analyze P&L statements; compile and maintain the accuracy of data related to payroll, AP/AR and delinquent accounts
(Note use of semicolon here.)

Utilize a PRECIS system in the tracking and updating of account prospect cards; provide full support to sales staff and compile weekly activity reports.

Experience in cost-effective purchasing of equipment directly from numerous manufacturers. Utilize Ashton-Tate software in the development of professionally-printed support materials.

Plan and implement sales concepts; develop specialized hardware and software promotions through interface with programmers and technical staff.

Effectively hire, train and supervise a staff of 12 in the prospecting, acquisition and management of key accounts in a large Midwestern territory.

Conducted in-depth research and wrote a comprehensive employee manual outlining worker benefits, disciplinary/probationary procedures and corporate philosophy.

Worked directly with restaurant owners, managers and construction contractors to meet specific equipment needs.
Conducted sales presentations, developed budgets and trained/supervised support personnel.

Responsible for effective customer service and the operation of a Wang computerized register at this high-volume drug store.

Power Words

Use these words to add power and impact to your writing:

Achieved	Delegated	Instituted	Recommended
Adapted	Demonstrated	Interpreted	Recruited
Administered	Designed	Introduced	Reduced
Advanced	Developed	Investigated	Reinforced
Advised	Devised	Launched	Reorganized
Allocated	Directed	Lectured	Researched
Amended	Drafted	Maintained	Restructured
Analyzed	Edited	Managed	Reversed
Appointed	Eliminated	Marketed	Reviewed
Approved	Established	Modified	Revised
Assigned	Evaluated	Monitored	Saved
Assisted	Expanded	Motivated	Scheduled
Authored	Expedited	Negotiated	Screened
Budgeted	Focused	Organized	(Re)Solved
Built	Forecasted	Participated	Streamlined
Calculated	Formulated	Performed	Strengthened
Collected	Founded	Pinpointed	Structured
Compiled	Generated	Planned	Supervised
Computed	Guided	Prepared	Supported
Conducted	Headed up	Processed	Tabulated
Contained	Identified	Produced	Taught
Controlled	Implemented	Promoted	Trained
Coordinated	Improved	Proposed	Trimmed
Created	Increased	Provided	Unified
Cut	Initiated	Published	Validated
Decreased	Innovated	Purchased	Wrote

4

NOTES ON FORMAT

Some Tricks of the Trade

Typesetting isn't the only way to get those nice "bullets" in your Experience section. Actually, it's done quite easily on a typewriter by using the small "o" and filling it in with a fine point pen. Ball point pens leave white spots, so make sure it has a small felt tip with black ink. I recommend hanging the bullet out in the margin as in the first example below, but you may also rest it above the second line of copy. Bullet points are great because they break up gray blocks of type, attract the eye and provide a focal point, which is followed by your most marketable skills and abilities:

EXPERIENCE:
- More than three years in software development including full responsibility for account acquisition, cost analysis, product installation and client relations.

- Effectively hire, train and supervise system analysts, programmers and data processing personnel.

- Fluent in COBOL and BASIC; familiar with PASCAL, FORTRAN, PL/1 and REXX.

You can also use a simple dash or asterisk:

    - Proven ability to increase vacuum cleaner sales through demographic research, targeted direct mail campaigns and door-to-door cold calling.

    * Field staff hiring, training and supervision; plan and conduct seminars on product benefits, sales presentations and professional closing techniques.

Always use frills like bold facing, underlining, italics, bullets, dashes or whatever *sparingly*. They should only be used to make major points stand out, or to set items apart and break-up type. They quickly lose their impact when overused. Another note on bolding, underlining or italicizing: avoid using all three in the same resume. Choose a combination of any two. My personal favorites are bolding and underlining, but pick whichever you prefer.

For a greater variety of overall visual formats, see pages 68, 80, 85, 130 and 170.

If you are using a typewriter and your full name is less than 15 letters, you can center your name at the top of the page and make it appear larger just by adding a space between letters:

R O B E R T E. J O N E S

instead of:

ROBERT E. JONES

Some of these techniques may seem simplistic. However, that is exactly why so few people think of using them, and find themselves with yet another boring data-sheet resume that doesn't work. Combining the techniques presented here will distance you from the pack and help you win the resume game.

Line Length

The resume examples in this guide follow a simple format. The body copy is almost always indented about two inches from the left margin. This allows for shorter lines and makes the resume more scanable, reducing reader fatigue. This also gives greater white space and an excellent place to put your **OBJECTIVE, EXPERIENCE** and other headings. Margins should be 1 inch all around, but they may be shortened to 3/4 inch or widened up to 1.5 inches as needed to fit your background neatly on one page if you just don't have enough information to start a second page. If you still need more or less space than margin shifting allows, change your type size by one-half point, but try to keep it at or near 11 points.

Avoid violating your margins or hyphenating words at the end of a line. However, you can make an exception to this rule for compound words such as self-employed, when the line ends after "self-". Don't worry about squaring-off (full justifying) your lines unless space is tight. You can fit more on the page when it's fully justified. Again, if you wish to hide employment gaps of 3-4 months, go ahead and use only years, but be prepared to back this up when asked. I prefer placement of dates directly across from job title or company name. You should begin your EMPLOYMENT descriptions with whichever title is most impressive. For example:

EMPLOYMENT: **Sales Manager** 9/88-Present

     <u>Rocker, Schnoocker & Fink,</u> Chicago, IL

However: <u>The State Department,</u> Washington, D.C. 3/87-Present
     Office Manager

Or: **The State Department,** Washington, D.C. 3/87-Present
     <u>Maintenance Man</u>

You should still underline Maintenance Man here because it clearly separates it from the copy which follows. Also, when dates are tucked-in to the right margin, they leave the left margin clear and allow for more white space.

Optical Centering

The optical center of a work of art, a resume, or just about anything, is roughly 1/3 down from the top of the page. It's the part of the page the eye likes looking at the most, and that's where your EXPERIENCE section will be:

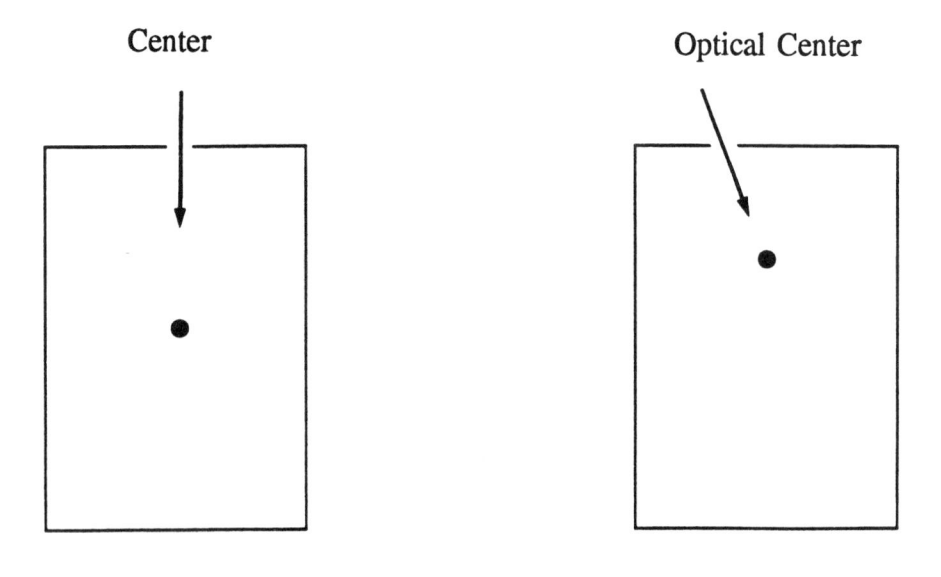

What Color Paper? White, off-white or ivory is best. Avoid dark grays, blues or browns. While these darker colors reduce glare from harsh office lights, they also reduce contrast between paper and ink. Avoid the splotchy parchment papers used by the large resume companies. Check the textured/linen designs such as Classic Laid Baronial Ivory, Howard Linen white (Aster) and one of the best, but hard to find resume papers, Strathmore Wove, in white or natural.

What typeface at what size? There are two basic styles of type: serif and sans serif. Serifs are the "tips" and "feet" at the top and bottom of letters. Almost every major newspaper uses serif type. What you are reading now is 12 point serif <u>Times Roman</u> bold and regular. Here is an example of sans (without) serif type:

This typeface is called <u>Helvetica</u> (also Univers & other names), in 12 pt.

This (serif) typeface is called <u>Times Roman</u> (or just Times) in 10 pt.

```
This (serif) typeface is called Courier in 10 pt. and is similar
to a common typewriter font.
```

Keep your typeface between 10 and 12 pts; 11 pt. is recommended. Use 12 pt. type only when necessary to fill the page. Anything smaller is hard for the eye to scan and anything bigger can seem pretentious. If all you have is a typewriter, make sure it has a plastic "one time" ribbon rather than an old cloth carbon ribbon. The difference in clarity is remarkable. The reproduction quality of masters printed on some of the newer typewriters rivals that of laser printers and typesetting. Many machines feature bold facing, interchangeable daisy print wheels and lift-off correction capabilities.

As for choosing between serif or sans serif types, serif types are recommended for most professions. They are easy to read, conservative and fairly common. If you are in a creative or high-tech field, i.e. advertising, graphic arts, aerospace technology or microchip development, a more modern sans serif type is recommended, such as Helvetica, Kent or New Gothic.

You can create an excellent resume master on a typewriter or PC and laser printer, and have it reproduced on a high-quality photocopier at a fraction of the cost of typesetting. This is recommended only if you need to save money and have access to good equipment. The typewriter should have proportional spacing, a feature which emulates typesetting because it actually "packs" the letters together, side-by-side. All typefaces used in this text are proportional (except Courier). The professionals I write for receive actual laser prints of their resume on their choice of paper (I usually recommend white linen). I can also provide them with a laser master on plain white paper to use for economical photocopying at a good quick-print shop, or they can get more laser prints on top-grade paper at three for $1.

If you can't find a good typist, typewriter or PC and laser printer, call the printers in your area. For about $40, they should be able to laser typeset your resume and give you at least 25 copies of a one-page format.

There are still "professional" resume services charging over $175 to write a one page resume and give you 25 copies. Some may still do it all on an electronic typewriter and a regular copy machine. Many of these services offer excellent help in marketing your skills on paper, but as mentioned earlier, writing quality varies widely. One company doesn't even represent itself as a resume company. They advertise "no professional fee" to "work with you" and have been known to charge more than $600 in "out-of-pocket" expenses. Again, if you decide to look into a professional resume service, make sure they advertise themselves as such, and offer a free consultation. Ask about the writer's background and see how long he or she has been writing resumes. Be sure to review the *writing* aspect of numerous samples, and don't pay more than

$175 for a full one-page writing project, with or without a cover letter. This should include a comprehensive interview on your abilities by the writer. For editing/re-writing or laser printing, expect to pay between $30 and $90 for a one page format, with at least ten laser prints or photocopies on quality paper. Before accepting your final prints, proofread your resume slowly and carefully. Check EVERYTHING, including dates of employment and the spelling of company names and your name & address.

Of course, this book is about writing your resume yourself, and you should be able to come close to professional writer's quality using the tips presented here. Typing your resume on an excellent typewriter with boldfacing, proportional spacing and lift-off correction ribbon can save you over $200 for a two-pager.

Don't forget secretarial and word processing services. They can key your resume onto a computer disk and laser print a master copy. Corrections and updates are then quick, easy and economical. If you can afford it, they can quickly laser print copies directly onto your paper choice. Another option is to have them print only a master on white paper and have that photocopied on to good resume paper.

- TIPSTER -

Beware of the black lines and gray streaks characteristic of many photocopies. These can sometimes be removed by lightening the exposure, but if you can't find a copier that works to your satisfaction, take it to a resume service or printer for actual laser prints or copies. Remember, this is your life's work, your career on paper. It must appear clean and crisp, with no clutter and as close to perfect as possible.

5

TOP SECRET RESUME EXAMPLES

The resume examples which follow were written by me for my clients. The first 12 of these resumes are annotated, with numbers and arrows pointing out what I believe are their most important elements. These numbers correspond to the notes below.

All of these samples were produced on a personal computer and laser printer. However, the first 12 use none of the extra design features offered by this equipment, such as small boxes (instead of bullets) or type fonts larger than 10 pt. (except those on pages 56, 58, 60 & 61). I did this to show that you can get these results on a regular typewriter at home, with the exception of the Helvetica typeface on a few of the samples.

Virtually all the other resume and letter examples are laser typeset in 11 pt. type, my favorite size. Remember that although some of the two-page resumes are printed on the front and back of a single sheet, you must never do this with your resume!

Feel free to use the best wordings and ideas from all these samples to create your own masterpiece. I've tried to include a good cross-section of resumes from various professions. I've also included several different methods for writing about particular items. These methods may at first seem to conflict, but they are simply different, effective ways of writing about your education, work experience, or abilities.

NOTATIONS: These notes correspond to the numbered arrows on resumes from pages 51 through 67:

Randall Kraft

(1) A specific OBJECTIVE to sell specific types of products. Change "food service industry" to your field: software, switches, fasteners, office equipment, etc. (2) A summary of all general areas throughout the years; the next three bullets are applicable to almost every major sales position. Pick the ones that apply to you and others pertaining to your goals. (3) Dollar volumes give Randall's talents power and potency, perhaps even making the reader jealous of previous employers. "Major Achievements" can be replaced by short outlines of company names and positions, when confidentiality isn't a major concern.

William Cosby

(1) A quick summary of the most common and important office activities and the equipment used to complete them. Second bullet begins immediately with people management skills. (2) Begin with the last and highest position attained at this resort. Because the OBJECTIVE is Office management, using reverse chronological places this Supervisory position at the top and grabs attention. Also, company name is placed above job titles, so that "Just Pants" company below acts as the umbrella above various positions. (3) Turns ordinary pack & ship work into an important, high-volume operation. (4) Shows importance and volume of work. Because the highest position obtained, Administrative Assistant, lasted only one month before his termination, we omitted dates at all three positions. (5) Covers lack of college degree.

John Walters

(1) Objective and Experience are kept short, with the major emphasis on actual employment for a position in Retail. (2) Shows willingness to work long hours, a virtual necessity in retail environments. (3) Backs up "profitability" in EXPERIENCE. (4) Spanish can be very useful in retail, especially with stockers and warehouse personnel. "Excellent communication skills" is optional, but here it helps fill-out the page, as does the layout of college course titles.

Steven A. Rogers

(1) No OBJECTIVE here, but it is implied with summary of "More than four years in..." Steven was emphasizing his experience in candidate interviewing and human resources. I made it a combination format and highlighted his experience in personnel, while downplaying his editing and writing background. (2) Shows ability to use previous writing experience in conjunction with recruiting. (3) "Temporary" explains brevity of the position. (4) Emphasis on developing job descriptions; explains brevity of position. (5) Name dropping of publications, with most important first, in this case
The Chicago Tribune.

Alice Shaminski

(1) A specific OBJECTIVE for a specific goal. Alice was submitting this resume to a committee for full-time Certified Teacher status. EXPERIENCE outlines total years of experience under various titles, and touches on types of subjects taught. (2) A short description because committee members already know her and what she does. (3) Lists degree, but more important, shows continuation of education after college to keep up with trends in PC instruction, and teaching of exceptional (LD) students. (4) Shows training in Spanish; though we intentionally omit that this was mostly during her high school years, it's important to include for a position at a language academy. This section also shows a strong interest in volunteer work and after-hours input. Additional note: dates omitted from Prior Experience as this was 14 years ago, so "One Year" is preferred.

Edward Vogts

(1) If you're a new college graduate, the best way to distance yourself from the pack is to include jargon of the field you've studied. This demonstrates a general knowledge of the industry and gives the impression you have a business-like mentality. (2) A good way to fill the page is to list your most relevant courses, and, even more importantly, any major term papers or research you completed. Did you do any research of local businesses and their practices? How did your course work prepare you for

the real business world? Explain it here. (3) This PERSONAL section helps fill the page and balances the stereotype of Accountants as number crunchers.

Bruce Wayne

(1) This is a great way to get attention and create an air of knowledgeability. As long as you have a background in these items, you can sometimes string these words together without stating your level of proficiency. But don't try this with more than one or two bullets, and always be honest! Never lie on your resume, because someday you will have to back it up. (2) Communication skills are important in any position, but especially in management. The ability to work with unions is prized. (3) Note layout of dates: first total time with the firm, then duration of specific positions. (4) LIFO/FIFO stands for last in/first out and first in/first out. Using the abbreviated form shows experience and projects Bruce at his proper level of expertise. (5) Important to show size of an otherwise unknown firm. (6) Shows initiative and leadership, as well as motivation to work himself through college by listing "100 percent of college costs." (7) Helps fill the page and could be deleted to save space.

Gregory Henson

(1) Shows knowledge of where to find information on businesses and how to use it effectively, which is a key talent in both product and service business leadership. (2) Outlines Greg's knowledge of computer systems and their application to banking activities. (3) Shows clear advancement and progression based on performance.

Clarence S. Darrow

(1) This OBJECTIVE can certainly be deleted if it's too limiting or if space is at a premium. Remember that specific objectives can always be stated in the cover letter once you've determined the needs and specialties of individual firms. (2) Due to lack of an EXPERIENCE section and the complexity of legal work, this job description should be fairly well detailed. But don't tell the reader everything about your position, just enough to leave them wanting to learn more about you and how you've accomplished these

goals: to meet the person behind the negotiations and government red tape. (3) Don't elaborate on something as simple as this position, just let them know the experience was worthwhile and helped pay for college. (4) Make this the umbrella above multiple degrees when possible and you avoid listing 1975 three times. Adds readability and reduces fatigue.

Debra Roberts

(1) Account acquisition is perhaps the most valuable sales skill -- and the ability to manage those accounts is a close second. (2) "high-energy sales" is unique and therefore gets attention. (3) Used to show reason for accepting temporary work rather than sales, which she was having trouble finding upon relocation. (4) Numbers are always valuable in Sales resumes, but don't overuse! (5) Downplay company ownership; some managers may think you have trouble taking orders, or will use their methods to start your own firm. (6) Long ago, so dates are omitted.

Robin Williams

(1) With the huge and sometimes confusing variety of computer positions, keep your OBJECTIVE as specific as possible. Remember they may be hiring for several computer-oriented positions simultaneously. (2) EXPERIENCE section here is optional, especially if you have more hardware, software or languages to list on the page. If such is the case, don't let EXPERIENCE push you into two pages. (3) This is the most important section, with previous positions and employers running a very close second. You can use qualifiers such as "fluent in" (languages) "familiar with," "proficient in," or "experience in". (4) Don't mention every project with your previous employers, just the most important ones with impressive clients such as NASA. Do try to touch on communication, presentation and client-relation skills whenever possible in order to stand above those who have only worked with bits and bytes. As in any field, remember that employers may require confidentiality about certain systems, designs and products. Be careful what you tell the competition.

Alfred E. Johnson

(1) Alfred was leaving the Navy in a few months to join the private sector. He needed something detailed to submit to technical staff at nuclear power stations, so I kept the summary short and moved quickly to hands-on duties and experience. (2) In a technical resume, write at a level your peers would appreciate.

NOTES ON RESUME EXAMPLES

1. Many of the resume examples which follow have margins smaller than 3/4 inch. I did this to add as much information as possible for use in your own resume, but you should always use at least 3/4 inch of white space on all sides of your resume text.

2. I've used both *percent* and % in these examples to show you how each appears. *Percent* is recommended in the Associated Press Style Book. The % sign is of course much shorter, and used more often in daily business operations. I therefore recommend % for your resume, though both are certainly acceptable.

RANDALL KRAFT

9878 West Arlington Street
Hoffman Estates, IL 60987

FUNCTIONAL
(See page 46 for explanation of arrows)

708/555-7654

OBJECTIVE:

(1)

Sales / Management
A position utilizing extensive experience in the sale of equipment and supplies to the food service industry.

EXPERIENCE:

(2)

- More than 14 years in the food service industry, including full responsibility for equipment sales, restaurant management and the setup and operation of new locations.

- Plan and conduct sales presentations in a professional manner; design and utilize sales support materials including videotapes, brochures and comprehensive user guides.

- Budget planning and sales forecasting; market research and new product introduction.

- Executive-level contract negotiation; experience in the use of CAD systems and the IBM XT in the development of equipment configurations to meet specific client needs.

- Sales staff hiring, training and motivation; interface with senior-level executives in the planning and implementation of sales incentive programs.

MAJOR ACHIEVEMENTS:

(3)

Marketing
Conducted in-depth regional market research and acquired exclusive rights to supply ovens, freezers and dishwasher equipment to a rapidly expanding chain of pizza stores.
Sales exceeded $1 million in the first six months. Projected sales for 1991: $4 million.

Management
Reduced turnover of Sales Representatives 30 percent at most recent position by improving training programs and compensation structures. Hired and trained an inside sales force of 19, exceeding all previous annual sales records in the Midwest for a leading food service firm.

Administration
Provided full interface between accounting and executive personnel in the design of a computerized order entry and billing system. Reduced delinquent accounts by 19 percent.

EDUCATION:

DePaul University, Chicago, IL
MBA, 1977

COMBINATION (REVERSE CHRONOLOGICAL)
(Arrows explained on pg. 46)

WILLIAM COSBY

687 Robert Lane　　　　　　　　　　Newton, IL 67488　　　　　　　　　　723/555-1730

OBJECTIVE:　　Office Management
A position where solid organizational skills would be utilized.

EXPERIENCE:

(1)
- Proven abilities in billing, inventory control, and order entry on IBM and WANG personal computers; familiar with Lotus 1-2-3, WordPerfect 5.0 and WordStar.
- Staff hiring, training, and supervision with solid communication skills; handle customer complaints and problems with tact and professionalism.

EMPLOYMENT:

(2) Indian Hills Resort, Bloomingdale, IL　　　　　　　　　　1980-1987
Assistant Supervisor
Trained and supervised one assistant in order entry and billing for this high-volume resort with ski lodge, restaurant and hotel.
Worked directly with the clientele: booked reservations, distributed keys and delivered phone messages in absence of regular front desk staff.
* Promoted to this position from Front Desk Clerk.
* Volume of positive customer response cards increased 20 percent in last two months as Assistant Supervisor.

Express Market Place, Elgin, IL　　　　　　　　　　1987-1988
Order Entry Assistant
(3) Utilized an IBM PC for order entry and the printing of customer invoices on a timely basis. Packed and shipped hundreds of individual orders via post office, UPS and various overnight carriers.

Just Pants Warehouse, Elgin, IL　　　　　　　　　　1988-Present
Earned promotions to three positions, most recent first:
Administrative Assistant, Corporate Office
Responsible for order entry, stock transfers and price code updates on a Wang terminal. Work directly with store managers to facilitate new openings. This entails stock procurement and the delivery of store fixtures.

Merchandising Representative, Corporate Office
Acted as liaison between managers of six stores and corporate directors.

Warehouse Representative
(4) Distributed bulk shipments to 54 stores nationwide.

EDUCATION:　　Elgin Community College, Elgin, IL　　　　　　　　　　5/88
(5) Successful completion of courses in English, Algebra I and Psychology

JOHN WALTERS   COMBINATION

234 Ash Street   (Arrows explained on pg. 46)
Park Forest, IL 60987   708/555-8154

OBJECTIVE: **Retail Sales Management**
                   A position where profit-building skills would be utilized.

EXPERIENCE: • More than 15 years in Retail Sales Management, with a proven ability to
(1)   increase bottom-line profitability.

EMPLOYMENT: **Assistant Manager-**   9/83-6/89
                   Zayre/Ames Corporation, Richton Park, IL
                   Effectively hired, trained, and supervised up to 23 employees in direct customer
                   service, sales and store maintenance/security.
                   In charge of budget planning and forecasting, sales reporting and cost-effective
                   stock procurement.

                   *   Utilized an NCR SAT/EPOS system for the storing and modification of data
                       related to advertisements.
                   *   Maintained accuracy of invoicing and billing; managed shipping/receiving and
                       worked with home office staff.
(2)   *   Occasionally worked nights during 24 hour grand openings.

(3)   *   Profits increased 15 percent to $640,000 on sales of $7.5 million.

                   Manager-   9/73-9/83
                   F.W. Woolworth, various Chicagoland locations
                   In charge of 14 employees and a lunch counter, with annual sales of $95,000.
                   Effectively managed stock ordering, inventory control and the layout of retail
                   displays.
                   Responsible for all sales, advertising coordination and office administration.
                   Communicated with vendors, suppliers and customers in a professional manner.

                   *   Profits increased 30 percent on sales of $600,000 annually.

EDUCATION: St. Xavier College, Chicago, IL   1975-1977
                   Successful completion of courses in:
                   - Business Management   - Sociology
                   - English   - Biology

                   *   Achieved ACT score of 26; Overall GPA: 3.4/4.0

                   Marist High School, Chicago, IL   1975
(4)   *   Earned State Scholarship

PERSONAL: Speak conversational Spanish;
                   Self-motivated, with solid communication and organizational skills.

(Arrows explained on pg. 47) STEVEN A. ROGERS *COMBINATION*

981 Golf Course Road Chicago, IL 60687 708/555-2524

EXPERIENCE:

(1)

* More than four years of combined experience in employee interviewing, recruiting and virtually all aspects of corporate human resources.

* Design forms for employee tracking and timely performance review; document disciplinary and counseling methods; work directly with trainers, staff and management in employee orientation, promotion and motivation.

EMPLOYMENT:

People Search, Inc., Itasca, IL 6/89-Present
Human Resources Representative
Responsible for recruiting and personnel activities at this recruitment research firm of 70 employees.
This is the largest firm in the world specializing in the compilation and sale of reports outlining qualifications of professionals in primarily high-tech fields.
Duties include employee counseling, file updating, and using WordPerfect and AREV software to track performance reviews and departmental succession plans.
Write/place advertisements and post jobs at numerous colleges and no-cost services. Monitor ad response and cost per hire.

(2)
- Planned and conducted over 180 interviews.
- Created and implemented seven new forms related to worker status and applicant interviewing.
- Conducted research and wrote/distributed a concise biography of this company for free inclusion in such publications as What Color Is Your Parachute?, The Macmillan Directory of Leading Private Companies, How To Get A Job In Chicago, and The Chicago Job Bank.
- Recognized by RA Supervisor for reducing turnover 18 percent in first three months.

Anderson Employment, Inc., Schaumburg, IL 9/88-6/89
Staff Writer

(3) Created this temporary position for myself. Authored resumes and job search materials on a referral basis for Anderson clientele. This provided an excellent opportunity to learn employment agency operations and recruitment methods.
Recruited from this position by People Search, Inc.
- Recognized by John Anderson for producing virtually capital-free revenues.

National Van Lines, Oak View, IL 2/88-9/88
Corporate Recruiter

(4) Accepted this six-month position to assist in recruiting and the relocation of National's corporate headquarters from Green Brook to Oak View.
- Recognized by Operations Management for providing over 50 qualified candidates for Service Rep and Fleet Coordinator positions, most of whom were hired.

STEVEN A. ROGERS   Page Two

Nuclear News, Des Plaines, IL   2/87-2/88
Assistant Editor
Solely responsible for final editing and proofreading of this newspaper which runs up to 42 pages and provides in-depth coverage of energy issues for legislators and business leaders worldwide.
- Researched and wrote a column entitled People In The News.
- Trained/supervised production staff and acted as liaison between writers and editors of the paper and all camera staff and printers.
- Selected and sized photographs, edited copy and assisted in layout; operated a dedicated MYCRO-TEK word processor and photo typesetter.

Professional Career Consultants, Chicago, IL   2/84-2/87
Writer and Branch Manager
Conducted comprehensive interviews with thousands of professionals and executives. Authored detailed job descriptions and worker profiles, up to four pages in length, for purposes of career placement.
- In charge of all operations at three offices; achieved highest production volume of five locations.
- Attained 99 percent client satisfaction through concise writing and effective customer service.

EDUCATION: Bachelor of Arts Degree   1983
                        Major: Journalism - Public Relations Emphasis
(5)   Northern Illinois University, DeKalb, IL

FREE-LANCE   Authored feature and news stories appearing in:
WRITING: The Chicago Tribune, Lerner/Voice Newspapers, Chicago Sounds Magazine, The Illinois Entertainer, The Xerox Centre Newsletter (Chicago Office), and the Public Relations Society of America Newsletter, (PRSA).

Alice Shaminski   COMBINATION
(Arrows explained on pg. 47)

1145 Marlboro Lane   Rolling Knolls, IL 60965   708/555-2415

(1) →   **ASSIGNED TEACHER CERTIFICATION**

EXPERIENCE:
- More than 12 years as Teacher, Full-Time Substitute and Instructional Aide, including full responsibility for lesson planning, material selection and performance evaluation.
- Utilize Macintosh PCs for teaching Mathematics, Social Studies and Computer Science to normal and learning disabled students.

EMPLOYMENT:

(2) →

Substitute, Full-Time Basis   1987-Present
St. Patrick Language Academy, Chicago, IL
Responsible for teaching intermediate grades.
Acted as Cadre Substitute for six months.

Instructional Aide - High School Section   1980-1987
Northwest Suburban Special Education Organization, Schaumburg, IL
Developed lesson plans and evaluated students.
Worked directly with the teacher in sourcing appropriate classroom materials and creating new student challenges.
* Utilized Apple PCs in a classroom environment for the instruction of Composition, Typing, Social Studies and Mathematics.

Prior Experience: **Teacher**   One Year
Bryant School and Lloyd School, Chicago Board of Education, Chicago, IL

EDUCATION:

University of Illinois, Champaign, IL
B.S. Degree, Elementary Education

(3) →

Northeastern Illinois University, Chicago, IL
Diagnosis and Remediation of Reading Problems, 1988
Personal computer use in the Classroom, 1987
The Exceptional Child, 1986

William Rainey Harper College, Palatine, IL
Completed a Word Processing course, with an emphasis on
WordPerfect and WordStar software, 1987.

(4) →

PERSONAL: Completed five year's training in Spanish; traveled in Spain, France and Italy.
Actively support the PTA. Secretary for the PPAC at Bryant School.
Seeking to volunteer for St. Patrick's proposed after school program.

COMBINATION / NEW COLLEGE GRADUATE

EDWARD VOGTS *(Arrows explained on pg. 47)*

176 Pistakee Drive
McHenry, IL 68697

815/555-2918

OBJECTIVE:	Accounting A position where comprehensive training and education would be utilized.
SUMMARY of QUALIFICATIONS: (1)	• Education in a full range of accounting functions, including accounts payable/receivable, inventory control and general ledger maintenance. • Familiar with Lotus 1-2-3 on the IBM PC, as well as word processing with WordPerfect 5.1 and WordStar. • Conduct speeches and presentations in a professional manner; reached state semifinal level as Debate Team member.
EDUCATION:	Northern Illinois University, DeKalb, IL **B.S. Degree** Graduated May, 1990 Major: Accounting Minor: Economics
(2)	Course work included experience in/with: -Statistical Process Control -AP/AR -Business Mathematics -Tax Accounting -Cost Analyses -Auditing -Payroll * President, Accounting Club, 1989 * Overall GPA: 3.4/4.0 * Self-funded 80% of college costs through part-time and Summer employment at: Green's Dry Cleaning, DeKalb, IL 1986-1990 **Bookkeeper/Sales Clerk** Assisted in manual bookkeeping at this busy store serving a community of 40,000. Handled general cash transactions using an electronic register. Maintained excellent rapport with customers and developed a repeat clientele.
PERSONAL: (3)	Energetic and self-motivated, with an excellent attention to detail and a high aptitude for figures. Enjoy skiing, cycling and jogging. Willing to travel or relocate.

BRUCE WAYNE *COMBINATION*
(Arrows explained on pg. 48)

8171 West Cave Lane
Gotham City, NY 19181   908/555-4320

OBJECTIVE: **Management:** A position utilizing professional talents in the set up and cost-effective management of Inventory Control and Purchasing systems.

EXPERIENCE: • More than 14 years of experience in inventory control, purchasing and the direction of internal logistics for major warehousing and distribution activities.

(1) ➤   • Budget planning and sales forecasting; general accounting, bookkeeping and cost analysis/reduction.

                       • Procedure development and system streamlining through comprehensive labor and cost analyses.

                       • Hire, train and motivate team leaders and supervisors; plan and implement worker incentive programs which have proven to reduce turnover while increasing worker morale and output.

(2) ➤   • Plan and conduct speeches and presentations; act as liaison between union leaders and corporate executives.

EMPLOYMENT: <u>Grove Fasteners,</u> Elk Grove Village, NY   1982-Present
                       Inventory Control Manager   1985-Present
(3) ➤   Manage an entire inventory of various distributed and manufactured goods, with stock consistently valued at over $31 million.
                       In charge of three crew supervisors; indirectly supervise 35 employees in warehousing, purchasing and distribution.

                       * Expedite delivery dates and generate status reports on using Lotus 1-2-3.
                       * Authorize customer credits, exchanges and all shipments exceeding $750,000.
                       * Successfully negotiated stock purchase and warehousing contracts with vendors and the clientele.
(4) ➤   * Initiated LIFO and FIFO programs resulting in faster deliveries worldwide.
                       * Reviewed entire base of raw product vendors and recommended new vendors as needed; this resulted in a savings of $18,000 in FY 1988.

                       Crew Supervisor   1982-1985
                       Effectively supervised a crew of ten stockers and forklift drivers in order picking, stocking, and truck loading/unloading.

                       * Assisted in improving warehouse layout, resulting in faster location of items.

BRUCE WAYNE   Page Two

                    Weber, Payne, Krebbs, Elk Grove Village, NY   1976-1982
                    Supervisor, Shipping and Receiving   1979-1982

Directly responsible for shipping and receiving functions for this manufacturer of electronic components for the personal electronics industry.

(5) →

* Annual sales in 1981: $14 million.
* Operated a Univac computer terminal in shipment/order tracking.
* Managed a crew of six including forklift drivers, truck drivers and stockers.

Shipping/Receiving Clerk   1976-1979

Gained excellent experience in order entry via telephone; communicated with the clientele on a daily basis.

Performed hand writing of customer invoices prior to assisting in conversion from manual to computerized operations.

* Voted Employee of the Month five times.
* Recognized by management for loyalty, drive and the ability to work well under pressure, according to annual performance reviews.

PRIOR EXPERIENCE: Self-funded 100% of college costs through employment at:

(6) →

Burger King, Syracuse, NY   1975-1976
Line Manager, Part-Time

Supervised a crew of 16 in customer service, order taking and cooking, in accordance with strict corporate guidelines.

* Promoted to this position from order taker and cook.

The Sharper Look, Syracuse, NY   1972-1975
Painter

Responsible for direct customer service and custom interior/exterior painting during weekends, holidays and Spring & Summer breaks.

EDUCATION: Upstate University, Syracuse, NY
B.A. Degree   Graduated 1976

Major: Business; Minor: Logistic and Inventory Management

* Graduated Cum Laude
* Dean's List, 1975

(7) →

Courses included experience in Basic Computer Operation, Statistics, Advanced Algebra and General Accounting.

GREGORY J. HENSON

982 Summerset Road
Schaumburg, IL 60948
708/555-9814

CHRONOLOGICAL
(Arrows explained on pg. 48)

EXPERIENCE:
- More than nine years in Finance, including full P&L responsibility for commercial credit lines at a major bank with over $30 million in assets.

- Hire, train and supervise loan officers and support personnel in product introduction and professional management of key accounts.

CAREER BACKGROUND:

Harris Bank, Schaumburg, IL — 1985-Present
Director, Commercial Finance — 1987-Present
In charge of the development and marketing of commercial credit lines to small and medium-sized firms in the Northwestern Suburbs.

(1) ➡ Analyze local industry trends and determine/meet client's specific business needs. Negotiate contracts with company principals and officers.
- Volume of new loans increased 21 percent, 1989.
- Dollar volume of new loans increased 18 percent, 1989.
- Manage two supervisors and indirectly, a staff of ten.

(2) ➡ - Assisted in the procurement and implementation of new computer hardware and software to speed computation and delivery of amortization schedules, resulting in greater client satisfaction as reflected in post sale surveys.

Loan Officer — 1985-1987
Responsible for loan origination and processing, including negotiations and the scheduling of capital assessments.
- Assisted in orienting new loan officers in account management and computer system operation.

Schaumburg Bank, Schaumburg, IL — 1981-1985
Loan Officer — 1983-1985

(3) ➡ Gained excellent experience in loan origination and client relations.
- Trained two employees in bank loan procedures and computer systems.

Personal Finance Counselor — 1983-1985
Counseled individuals and assisted in meeting their long- and short-term business goals.

Teller — 1981-1983

EDUCATION:
Northwestern University, Evanston, IL — Graduated Cum Laude, 1981
B.A. Degree, Finance and Administration Minor: Economics
* Elected President of the Finance and Banking Club, 1980.

CLARENCE S. DARROW *CHRONOLOGICAL*
(Arrows explained on pg. 48)

124 East Chestnut #243
Chicago, IL 60698
312/555-9876

OBJECTIVE: A position utilizing an extensive background in Administrative Law.
(1)

CAREER
BACKGROUND: United States Department of Education, Office for Civil Rights, Chicago, IL
2/80-Present
Attorney/Advisor
Primarily involved in civil rights compliance determinations, providing advice and analyses for the planning and execution of investigations related to virtually all types of discrimination.

(2)

Responsible for tracing funds utilized by various agencies and programs receiving federal assistance; negotiate directly with agency officials and interpret/enforce federal guidelines.

- Accept full-charge responsibility for numerous enforcement proceedings.
- Determine jurisdiction for specific cases.
- Review applications for federal funds.
- Assigned as Coordinating Attorney for regional technical assistance related to statutes enforced by the U.S.D.E. office for Civil Rights.

As Law Librarian, effectively manage a 2000 volume library for U.S.D.E./O.C.R./C.R.A.S.-v personnel.
- Train colleagues in the use of Westlaw's computerized legal research system.
- Organize quarterly case sessions.
- Monitor activities in bureaus and federal courts on a daily basis for all department attorneys and staff.

Private Law Practice, Miami, FL   1978-1980
Attorney
Responsible for a full range of civil matters, including estates, trusts, and wills.
Acted as consultant to Dean of the Miami School of Law in the assessment of public services.

University of Miami School of Law, Miami, FL   1971-1978
Assistant Law Librarian
(3) Gained an excellent background in the layout and operation of law libraries.
Directly involved in the research of potential new acquisitions.

CLARENCE S. DARROW Page Two

Law Clerk Experience:

<u>Louis Dartell,</u> Miami, FL Oct.-Nov. 1978
<u>Flynn, Peters, and Havelcheck,</u> Miami, FL Fall, 1976

EDUCATION: <u>University of Miami School of Law,</u> Miami, FL

J.D., Graduated Cum Laude 1978

- Ranked among the top 20 percent.
- Listed in Who's Who in American Colleges and Universities.
- Dean's List, four semesters.
- Earned Book Award for Civil Procedure I, as well as for Workmen's Compensation Certificate of Merit, Student Bar Association.

(4) ➡ Degrees Earned, 1975, Each Magna Cum Laude and General Honors:

A.B., Major: Politics and Public Affairs Minor: History
B.S., Major: Mathematics Minor: Computer Science
B.G.S., Major: Religion

- National Mock Trial Member, one year.
- Law School Representative on U.M. Health Center Advisory Board.
- U.M. Delegate to O.D.K. National Convention and Province III Convention, two consecutive years.
- Board Member and Liaison to U.M. Administration, U.M. Student Government.
- Member, Client Counseling Board, one year.
- Director, Student Bar Book CoOp.

(Arrows explained on pg. 49)   **DEBRA ROBERTS**   *COMBINATION*

897 Salem Trail #B2   Northbrook, IL 60687   708/555-3827

OBJECTIVE:

(1)

Inside Sales
A position where proven abilities in account acquisition and management would be utilized.

EXPERIENCE:

(2)

- More than six years in high-energy sales including full responsibility for cold calling, market penetration and the successful development of major accounts.

- Handle staff training and supervision in telephone prospecting, product lines and professional client relations.

EMPLOYMENT:

(3)

Sales / Customer Service   12/89-Present
Salem Temporary Service, Deerfield, IL
A full range of activities include customer service, order taking and telephone sales at two large suburban companies.
Accepted these positions upon relocation from Omaha, Nebraska.

Nebraska Sales Representative   1/86-12/89
Jones License and Title Service, Palos Hills, IL
Developed a major Nebraska territory through telephone and in-person cold calling of transportation firms and currency exchanges.
Acquired numerous accounts and maintained solid, profitable relationships with existing accounts in Iowa and Nebraska.
Processed title transactions and administered invoicing, collections, and daily bank deposits.

(4)

* Dramatically increased client base from 2 to 96.

Sales Representative   1/86-12/89
Bingo King, Council Bluffs, IA
Responsible for planning and implementing sales concepts and acquiring/maintaining profitable accounts in a three-state Midwestern region. Products included bingo paper and equipment marketed to mid- and upper-level wholesalers.

* Effectively trained sales representatives in presentations, up-selling and personalized client relations.
* Personally increased monthly sales from $100,000 to $200,000.

Marketing Representative   5/83-12/84
National Econotel, Omaha, NE
Promoted to this position from Inside Sales Representative.

DEBRA ROBERTS   **Page Two**

Generated leads via telephone; called on virtually all types of professionals for the sale of long distance telephone services.
Designed sales proposals, maintained a solid customer base and a high closing ratio.

*   Consistently met or exceeded sales quota of $18,000/month.

(5) ➤ **Owner / Operator**   11/77-4/83
The Nail Lady, Hinsdale, IL

In charge of all sales, marketing and administrative functions at this nail sculpture and electrolysis shop.

Buyer   5/79-6/82
Eye On Design, Hinsdale, IL
Responsible for customer service, correspondence and the design/purchase of jewelry for a discriminating clientele.

EDUCATION: Moraine Valley Community College, Palos Hills, IL
Nursing Program, completed two years.

(6) ➤ Accurate College of Hair Removal, Hinsdale, IL
Successful completion of Certification Course.

Luther South High School, Chicago, IL
Graduate

ROBIN WILLIAMS

COMBINATION
(Arrows explained on pg. 49)

1652 South Eastwood Avenue
Chicago, IL 60698

708/555-1832

OBJECTIVE:

(1)

A position in Systems Programming where diverse professional skills would be utilized.

EXPERIENCE:

(2)

- More than five years in systems programming, including the development of tractable user procedures and manuals.

- Provide system documentation and full application support at client locations.

(3)

Hardware:
IBM 3033, 370/158, 360/145 and 360/30; Honeywell 437; Univac; Prime 850 and CDC 160-A.

Software/Languages:
Proficient in COBOL and Fortran; familiar with BAL, JCL, BASIC, Assembler and Pascal "C". Operating systems include UNIX, OS/MVS and APPLE II DOS.

EMPLOYMENT:

Systems Programmer   1987-Present
Unitex, Inc., Chicago, IL

(4)

Responsible for new program design and production for this major supplier of data processing services to NASA.
Installed and maintained OS/MVS on an IBM 360/145.
Trained and supervised software personnel on system modifications.

* Successfully converted UNIX from IBM 3033 to client's Honeywell 437.
* Directly involved in the preparation and submission of a proposal which was accepted by a major automobile manufacturer in Detroit, MI.

Systems Programmer   1985-1987
Ameribell, Inc., Houston, TX

Involved in the development of telecommunications systems on Univac and Prime mainframes using BAL, JCL, and BASIC.

EDUCATION:

Northern Illinois University, DeKalb, IL
B.A. Degree, Computer Programming   1985
   * Dean's List, 1984

Computer Science courses included:
- Operating Systems   - Computer Architecture
- Data Structures   - Discrete Structures

   * Utilized the IBM 3033, 370/158, Honeywell 437 and CDC 160-A.

ALFRED E. JOHNSON
560 Ridge Drive
Bartlett, IL 60313
708/555-7812

COMBINATION
(Arrows explained on pg. 50)

OBJECTIVE: A position with a consulting or engineering firm where experience in nuclear systems maintenance and operations would be utilized.

SUMMARY:

(1)

- Experienced in reactor plant operations and maintenance; supervise modification & repair work and establish special plant conditions.

- Skilled in personnel supervision, training and evaluation; assist in work scheduling and training program development and implementation.

EXPERIENCE: *United States Naval Officer* 1985-Present
Nuclear Qualified Surface Warfare Officer
Nuclear Officer Programs Manager, Navy Recruiting District Chicago, Carbondale, IL
9/88-Present

Responsible for recruiting outstanding engineering and science students from top universities and colleges for the Navy's nuclear surface and submarine officer training programs.
- In charge of all program budgeting, planning, advertising and direct mail activities for one of the largest recruiting districts in the country.
- Responsible for interviewing and technical evaluation/screening of applicants.
- Selected for promotion to Lieutenant Commander.

Main Propulsion Assistant, USS California (CGN 36), San Francisco, CA   9/87-9/88

Qualified as Engineer by the Naval Reactors Division of the U.S. Department of Energy. Managed 60 personnel, two divisions and four work centers as Propulsion Assistant.

- Served as Main Control Engineering Officer of the watch during general quarters and special operations.
- Served as Tactical Action Officer, responsible for ship's sensor and weapons while deployed to the North Arabian Sea and Persian Gulf operating areas.
- Served as ship's Safety Officer, Officer in Charge of the Ship's Damage Control Training Team and Senior Drill Monitor for the ship's Nuclear Training Team.

(2)

- As Nuclear Work Coordinator, scheduled, coordinated and managed steam plant and reactor plant mechanical systems maintenance and repair, specifically:
- Two ion exchange resin and purification filter media discharge and refill evolutions.
- Five reactor coolant loop drain, evacuation and fill operations to support reactor coolant pump modifications.
- Numerous reactor plant primary valve repairs and subsequent system hydrostatic tests.
- Steam generator u-tube eddy-current testing, tube pulls and closeout inspections.
- Primary and secondary system relief valve adjustment and testing.
- Main feed pump and main circulation pump overhauls and replacement.

ALFRED E. JOHNSON — Page Two

Operations and Deck Division Officer, USS Nimitz CVN-68,
Mayberry, VA 3/85-9/87

- Ranked #1 of eleven Junior Lieutenants on board.
- Responsible for managing two divisions (approximately 40 personnel).
- Qualified Officer of the Deck Underway.
- Qualified Tactical Action Officer, responsible for employment of the ship's sensors and weapons systems.
- Top Secret Clearance based on Special Background Investigation.

HONORS:
* Awarded Navy Commendation Medal for superior performance in supervising Nuclear work during USS California's Drydocking.
* Awarded Navy Achievement Medal for superior performance in supervising emergent propulsion plant repairs while USS California was deployed to the Indian Ocean.
* Awarded Navy Achievement Medal for superior performance as departmental maintenance and material officer during USS Nimitz overhaul.

EDUCATION:
B.S. Degree, Nuclear Engineering, June 1982
Northern Illinois University, DeKalb, IL

Navy Nuclear Power Training
Rantail, IL, FL/West Milton, N.Y.
Completed comprehensive graduate-level program in the theory, design and operation of naval nuclear reactors.
Qualified to supervise operation of a naval nuclear reactor plant under normal and emergency conditions.

Mr. Terry Motley

1460 S. Fairlane #112
Schaumburg, IL 60193

708/894-1327

CREATIVE WRITING, DESIGN AND ILLUSTRATION

Experience:
- ❏ More than two years in professional writing, design and illustration, including full responsibility for creative development, execution and prompt client servicing.

- ❏ Successful experience in virtually all aspects of creative writing, design and/or development for:
  - ☞ **T.V., Radio, Newspaper, Magazine and Point-Of-Purchase advertising for major clients...**
  - ☞ **Corporate Logos, Slogans & Tag Lines...**
  - ☞ **3-D/Graphic Designs of all types, especially for Brochures, Newsletters and Trade Show Themes...**

Employment:

Free-lance Copywriter and Artist   Present
Responsible for creative writing and design of a wide range of promotions for radio, cable & regional T.V., 3-D P.O.P. displays and specialty logos.

- ☞ Major accounts include Up, Up and Away, created and executed near life-size illustrations of NBA Basketball stars.
- ☞ Created & executed a logo for Universal West Land Developers.

Prior Experience:

Copywriter/Artist Lane and Associates, Naperville, IL
Performed writing and design work for radio spots, print ads, 3-D work, brochures, newspaper items and full advertising campaigns.

Copywriter/Artist Bertram Marketing Resources, Warrenville, IL
Wrote/designed T.V. and radio ads, slogans and tag lines, designs & Illustrations, brochures, newsletters and magazine ads.
Developed 3-D materials, a sales office design and T.V. and radio ads used by such clients as Sears, Subway and a major Tinley Park land developer.

Designer St. Clair Pakwell, Bellwood, IL
Projects included development of trade show themes, brochures, boxes and bags.

Education & Professional Affiliations:

Ray College of Design
Three-Year Associate Degree: Advertising Design
Bachelor's Degree Expected 1994.
GPA: 3.5/4.0.

Portfolio Available Upon Request

Notes: A very unique design for a creative illustration, design and/or writing position. Terry would take any of the three. We cut this page just within the dotted line to fit perfectly in a personalized, 6"x9" enveloped printed with his eye-catching artwork. The lines, pointing hands and 3-D squares on top were created with **PageMaker 4.0**, a desktop publishing program available for your DOS or Macintosh computer, and used by some print and resume shops. The Experience section avoids repetitition under each job. We used the jargon of the industry, though sparsely. Terry used "Mr." because he would often be mistaken as female prior to interviews. He suggested I use his real name and address here, so I did.

ARTHUR D. WOOD

COMBINATION

190 Stove Lane #F
Glenview, IL 61025

708/555-5069 Res.
708/555-5088 Bus.

OBJECTIVE: **Management**
A position in the Tool and Die industry where proven hands-on business skills would be utilized.

EXPERIENCE:
- Full project management abilities include production scheduling, SPC/quality control and cost containment.

- Experience in staff hiring, training and supervision; effective in job delegation and maintaining positive worker motivation and morale.

- Assist in developing and updating policies related to worker and management relations.

- Experience in JIT delivery and cost-effective inventory control.

- Proven ability to increase sales with new and existing clientele, through professional communication techniques.

EMPLOYMENT: G.E.C. Industries, Inc., Wheeling, IL   8/87-Present
Plant Manager
In charge of all operations related to metal stamping, tool and die work, progressive dies, jigs and fixtures -- from initial concept to finished product.
Machine line includes punch presses up to 300 ton capacity to produce complex metal parts.

Consistently schedule, revise, and improve production lines; handle temporary, small tooling and troubleshooting.

Train and supervise up to 20 employees; schedule work hours; maintain pay rates that are fair to workers and profitable for management.

- Constantly seek to improve working conditions and worker morale through review and upgrading of corporate policies.
- Commended for reducing annual production costs 12 percent.

Arthur D. Wood   Page Two

J.B. Tool Co., Elk Grove, IL   9/83-8/87
Contract Tool and Die Maker
Produced tools and dies on a contract basis.
Specialized in class "A" work on a wide variety of products.

Keats Manufacturing Company, Evanston, IL   4/78-9/83
Tool and Die Maker
Established new cost-cutting methods for tool and die fabrication, including the introduction of lower- priced materials.

- Implemented a new procedure which lessened die wear due to sharpening.
- Significantly increased product quality through production and product tracking methods.
- Directly responsible for improving design standards, as well as a 50 percent decrease in production downtime.

Celco Tool and Engineering, Schiller Park, IL   3/71-4/75 and 6/76-4/78

Diemaker
Assumed responsibilities of owner and manager during vacations and absences.

- Acted as Group Leader for more than 50 percent of all projects in which I was involved.

Previous Employment at shops in the Chicago area, including Remcel Engineering, Tauber Brothers Tool Company and Kamen Tool and Engineering.

EDUCATION: Evanston Junior Community College, Evanston, IL
Completed courses in Liberal Arts
- Successful completion of numerous industry-related courses, seminars and workshops.

JUDY SAMOZA   COMBINATION

2902 W. Eugenie #2S
Chicago, IL 60614   312/555-3421

OBJECTIVE: **NURSING:** A position where diverse, professional RN talents would be utilized.

EXPERIENCE:
- More than six years in comprehensive patient care, including full Emergency Unit responsibilities.

- Plan and conduct staff and patient in-services in a professional manner; organize data on hospital computer systems and utilize charts, graphs and WordPerfect software.

- Experience in prompt, accurate assessments and personalized patient care; proven ability to work with physicians and staff at all levels of experience.

EMPLOYMENT: St. James Hospital, Park Forest, IL   6/88-Present
Staff RN, Emergency Unit
Responsible for up to 50 patients per shift in a busy, 20-bed unit.
As triage nurse on a staff of six nurses, stabilize patients, execute critical decisions and handle a steady flow of patients.
* Receive up to 40 trauma patients per shift.

Cook County Hospital, Chicago, IL   3/86-6/88
Staff RN, Emergency Unit

Effectively treated numerous gunshot and motor vehicle accident trauma patients at this extremely busy 14-bed unit
* Performed comprehensive training of nursing students. Subjects included IV therapy, CPR and ER patient assessment methods.
* Supervised an outpatient methadone treatment program.
* Acted as mobile intensive care nurse from an ambulance; interfaced with an EMT and respiratory therapist.

Kishwaukee Hospital, Sycamore, IL   2/84-3/86
Staff RN, Emergency Unit

Gained comprehensive ER experience in a 15-bed ER unit.

EDUCATION: Loyola University, Chicago, IL
B.S.N. - Nursing   1983
GPA: 3.5/4.0

Emergency Medical Technician Certificate   1983

MICHELLE A. CRACKERS *DETAILED CHRONOLOGICAL*

6740 North Hoyne   Chicago, IL 60689   312/555-8873

EXPERIENCE: **PUBLICITY / PROMOTION ASSOCIATE**
Sparrow-Conant Corporation, Chicago, IL   12/86-Present
Marketing: Coordinate production for product packaging and sales promotional materials. This involves detailed copy writing and editing under strict deadlines.

Public Relations: Established national product publicity program for retail line of audio programs. Developed communications tactics, worked with best-selling authors and supervised creation of print and radio media lists to gain article placements in the nation's top 15 markets.
Media placed in *USA Today, Ladies Home Journal, The Chicago Tribune* and *The Oakland Tribune.*
* Coordinated a trade-for-mention program with the top-ranked radio station in Chicago; garnered $8,000 worth of promotional air time.
* Assisted with press party and publicity for a video with Chicago Cub Andre Dawson.
* Responsible for trade media relations. Efforts resulted in 12 placements in a leading industry publication, including 14 product reviews in 1987.

Advertising: Plan and implement trade and direct response print advertisements.

Special Events: Coordinated key customer breakfasts with authors at trade shows.

PUBLIC RELATIONS MANAGER
Evanston Commons Association, Evanston, IL   7/84-4/86
A non-profit social service agency with 12 facilities throughout Chicago.
Management: Developed and managed all events for ECA's 90th Anniversary Celebration, including writing the president's speech and organizing a dinner and dance. Acted as association liaison to two board of director's committees.

Special Events: Worked directly with board members in the coordination of a gala "Birthday Party." Successfully organized an Anniversary year festival for service recipients, and the "What I Like Best About My Neighborhood" Children's Art Contest. Personally secured WLS-TV as co-sponsor.
* Generated publicity resulting in 3.8 million media impressions.
* Gained underwriting from Southland Corporation for two consecutive years for the Christmas Cheer Dinner Giveaway.
* Arranged the distribution of 300 dinners to the needy.

Marketing: Supervised the fall direct mail solicitation campaign and increased contributions by 23 percent over the previous year.

Media Relations: Responsible for more than 30 print placements in major publications including *The Washington Post*.

Publications / Special Projects: Performed writing, editing and production supervision for a special anniversary annual report and various newsletters.
* Writer of the winning entry in the United Way/Rothschild Heart of Gold Award Program for outstanding community volunteers.

ASSISTANT TO REGIONAL SALES/MARKETING MANAGER
Reader's Digest Services, Inc., Chicago, IL   10/82-6/84
Marketing: Assisted in writing and preparing a six-month sales/marketing plan and comprehensive sales reports.
Handled full coordination of assignments between corporate office, regional manager and six field sales representatives.
* Initiated a sales promotion with the district manager and boosted sales 10 percent.

Media Relations: Worked with district managers and facilitated local media relations and special issue presentations.

PROFESSIONAL ACTIVITIES: Women in Communications, Inc.: As General Chairperson of the 22nd Annual Career Conference, increased corporate supporters from seven to 17.
Hugh O'Brian Youth Foundation: Public Relations Director for the Illinois State Leadership Seminar for outstanding high school sophomores, 1986.
Program Committee Member: International Assoc. of Business Communicators, 1987.

EDUCATION: Northern Illinois University, DeKalb, IL
Bachelor of Arts Degree   1982
Major: Journalism / Public Relations   Minor: Political Science
* Self-funded 100 percent of college costs.
* Free lance experience included:
  Contributing Editor: *Fulfillment* magazine, a glossy monthly publication produced by The Signature Group.
  Writer: *The Near East Gazette*. Gained front-page position with news reporting on controversies surrounding local real estate developments.
  Consultant: The Children's Home & Aid Society of Illinois. Provided creative services for the 1986 annual report.

HONORS & INTERNSHIPS: Received the George M. Crowson Outstanding Senior in Public Relations Award -- The Public Relations Society of America, (PRSA) 1981.
National Citation For Outstanding Chapter Service, The Public Relations Student Society of America, (PRSSA) 1981.
President, PRSSA, Northern Illinois University Chapter.
Intern: The Burson-Marsteller, Inc. Professional Partners Program.

Catherine M. Myerski

826 Elgin Lane
Geneva, IL 69483

CHRONOLOGICAL

708/555-3821

OBJECTIVE: Product Management
A position where diverse technical skills would be utilized.

EMPLOYMENT: <u>Nuclear Sources, Inc.,</u> Scoreville, IL   10/87-Present
Product Manager
Responsible for the direction of new product planning and development activities.
Create and implement comprehensive marketing strategies and plans -- as well as budgets for media and product introduction materials.
Plan and conduct competitive product and market share analyses.
Research, produce and update catalogs and price lists.

- Provide full support in the training of sales personnel.
- Developed a detailed product cost and selling price spreadsheet.

<u>Cerebral Business Systems,</u> Schaumburg, IL   9/85-10/87
Product Line Manager - Payment Systems Division
Completely responsible for the preparation of marketing plans for new credit authorization terminals.
Designed innovative advertising/promotional literature, including slides and trade show exhibits.

- Authored comprehensive system programming, installation and operation manuals.
- Developed and successfully implemented customer training programs.
- Directly involved in the research and development of new products, including the planning, coordination and testing of future software releases.

<u>NGC Home Electronics,</u> Highhill, IL   7/83-10/85
Peripheral Product Coordinator
Produced NGC MultiSync monitor -- including research of market potential and preparation of a comprehensive marketing plan.
Evaluated pre-production printers and monitors for performance and specification compliance.

- Researched and wrote detailed, annotated operational manuals.
- Established a product tracking system for entire sales force.

EDUCATION: B.S. Degree: Marketing   Graduated 5/83
<u>University of Arizona,</u> Tempe, AZ
- President of business administration student council
- Elected as Honors Convocation Speaker and Emcee for the Business College.

AFFILIATIONS: Phi Chi Theta Professional Fraternity Member; American Marketing Association.

BETTY WHITE	*COMBINATION*

130 3rd Avenue N.W.
Seattle, WA 98176   206/555-0257

OBJECTIVE   **Legal Secretary:** A position where professional skills would be utilized.

EXPERIENCE
- Proven abilities as Secretary and Receptionist, including research, correspondence writing, direct client relations and payroll processing.

- Familiar with WordPerfect and the IBM Memorywriter, as well as various switchboard systems; compile and produce detailed reports via dictaphone and work effectively with legal staff.

- Handle general accounting, bookkeeping and special projects.

EMPLOYMENT   *McKenzie-Brackman, Attorneys,* Seattle, WA   7/90-Present
Legal Secretary
A full range of responsibilities include assisting in case studies and the preparation/updating of legal documents.
Operate a 14-line switchboard; handle general reception of clientele and typing of correspondence related to legal matters.

Seattle, WA   4/83-7/90
Homemaker

The Seattle Bank   11/79-4/83
Payroll Clerk   4/80-4/83
Maintained accuracy of over 400 time cards and processed computer input forms and reports.
Utilized MSA and ADP computer systems, as well as Addressograph equipment.

- Scheduled data processing projects and checked/distributed pay stubs; processed salary changes and updated life insurance cards.
- Developed microfilm and typed/produced monthly life insurance reports; processed employee's Savings Bonds.

Receptionist/Secretary   11/79-4/80
Primarily responsible for letter and memo typing from Dictaphone and rough drafts.
Worked directly with senior-level personnel on special projects.

EDUCATION   *Griffin College,* Seattle, WA
Completion of Legal Secretary Program   Diploma, 1985

SYLVESTER BRIDGES   COMBINATION
9291 Shaver Drive
Barrington, IL 60090
708/555-6858

SALES / SALES MANAGEMENT

EXPERIENCE

- More than 16 years in sales and sales management, including proven success with leading manufacturing firms in major metropolitan markets.

- Handle comprehensive research and competitive analysis for the implementation of strategic marketing plans.

- Assist in staff training and supervision with excellent communication skills; develop a strong "team" atmosphere among sales reps and support personnel.

- Determine and meet client's specific business needs; plan and conduct sales presentations with key clientele in a personalized, professional manner.

- Demonstrated success in the development of long-term business partnerships.

EMPLOYMENT

Flasho Manufacturing, Minneapolis, MN   1987-Present
Midwest District Sales Manager   1988-Present
Responsible for sales to mass merchants for this home textile marketer which has a national client base generating $100 million annually. Work directly with merchants at major chains, department stores, supermarkets and drug stores.
Manage budgets, determine sales quotas and penetration strategies and monitor co-op advertising efforts on a regular basis. Effectively train and supervise a broker sales force and various company representatives.

* Personally handle major accounts including J.C. Penney, Walgreens, Kohls, Osco Drug, Pamida, Shopko, Meijers, and Cotter & Company,
* Increased sales from $800,000 to $3.5 million, 1987-Present.
* Established productive relationships with major accounts resulting in a dramatic rebound in the Midwest territory.
* Hired and trained a new sales representative for Program Selling in Indianapolis. This resulted in a dramatic sales increase for a previously dormant territory.
* Promoted to this position from **Senior Midwest Account Executive**, 1987-1988.

The Bale Company, A division of Sears Roebuck, Hackensack, NJ   1984-1987
Chicago Regional Sales Manager   1985-1987
Management duties included the development of buying plans and sales forecasts for this manufacturer of intimate apparel.

* Trained and supervised four sales associates & field merchandisers working with major accounts such as K-Mart, Carson Pirie Scott and other retailers.

SYLVESTER BRIDGES	Page Two

Key Account Sales Representative - Chicago / Milwaukee 　　　　　1984-1985
Responsible for key account sales to major department stores.
Maintained direct communication with buying staff and senior store management regarding volume and profitability.
Trained and supervised three sales associates.

Harold Rice & Associates, Niles, IL 　　　　　1983-1984
Account Executive
Called directly on national advertisers to plan and implement marketing and communication programs.
Worked primarily with point-of-purchase displays and package designs, as well as sales promotions and related materials.

Playtex, Inc. New York, NY 　　　　　1981-1983
Key Account Sales Representative - Chicago / Milwaukee
Responsible for the sale of branded product lines to major department stores, as well as specialty and military accounts. Presented national promotions for new products and programs.
Developed/implemented effective buying plans and generated monthly reorders.
Supervised one merchandiser and maintained excellent communications with key accounts.

* Instrumental in launching marketing campaigns which increased sales and service demands.
* Acted as liaison between company and accounts to provide timely information, expedite service and resolve conflicts.
* Increased sales volume 12 percent, 1981-1983.

Ralph Meyers Intimate Apparel Company, Inc. New York, NY 　　　　　1973-1981
Field Sales Representative
Conducted high-volume sales to major department stores, as well as military and specialty accounts.
Involved in all phases of direct sales, including program development, inventory control and customer relations.

* Recognized for excellent sales performance.
* Increased sales volume in last assigned territory by $315,000.

EDUCATION

Northeastern University, Chicago, IL
Bachelor of Arts Degree / Marketing 　　　　　1973

Xerox Corporation
Completed Selling Skills II Course 　　　　　1984

PERSONAL

Willing to travel extensively; willing to relocate.

JOHN S. RAZZ

2751 Autumn Road East
Salem, OR 94305

CHRONOLOGICAL

512/555-6765 Res.
512/555-8590 Bus.

EXPERIENCE:

Executive Director — 1989-Present
<u>Christians for Youth Initiatives,</u> Eugene, OR
In charge of all activities for this non-profit organization providing resources and training nationwide for children 11-14 years of age.

Area Manager — 1988
<u>Alpha Products, Inc.,</u> Salem, OR
Managed sales and marketing for this manufacturer of security systems and real estate lock boxes.

Associate Director of University Relations — 1983-1987
<u>William University,</u> Salem, OR
Coordinated fund raising programs for Mark O. Hatfield Library, centerpiece of a $22.5 million capital campaign.
Promoted to this position from **Director of Alumni Relations**.

Assistant to the Vice President — 1981-1982
<u>The University of South Carolina,</u> Columbia, SC
Authored proposals and conducted research for cooperative programs between the University, the State of South Carolina, private industry, the federal government and foreign countries.

Legislative Assistant — 1976-1981
<u>U.S. Senator Mark D. Rogers,</u> Washington, DC
Acted as director and advisor to the Senator on issues including education, defense, transportation and world hunger.
Prepared speeches, floor statements and background papers, as well as appearances on behalf of Senator Mark Rogers.
Acted as office liaison to individuals and groups in Oregon seeking action or assistance from U.S. government departments.

* Served as campaign Field Director for the Committee to Re-Elect Mark O. Hatfield in the Senator's successful senate race of 1978.
* Gained hands-on experience in public speaking and the writing, preparation and distribution of correspondence, promotional materials, and mass mailings.
* Planned itineraries in compliance with state and local regulations.

Internship — 1976
<u>The Dixie Endowment of Indianapolis, IN</u>
Conducted research and program evaluation in the Divisions of Education and Religion.
Directly involved in projects related to values and the liberal arts, as well as in various religion-oriented activities and programs.

Student Member 1975
The Oregon Educational Council, Salem, OR
Appointed by the Governor of Oregon, and confirmed by the State Senate to serve as the first student member of the Oregon Educational Coordinating Council with full voting privileges.
This council is charged with the coordination planning and evaluation of Oregon's educational system.

College Admissions Representative Summers, 1974-1975
Warner Pacific College, Salem, OR
Conducted speeches and contacted/counseled prospective students.
Traveled to youth camps, conventions and churches throughout the United States and Canada.

EDUCATION:

M.Ed. Degree 1982
Graduate degree in Higher Education Administration
Student Personnel Services
University of Carolina, Columbia, SC

B.A. Degree 1975
Major: Religious Studies
* Elected student body President, senior year
Warner Pacific College, Salem, OR

Volunteer Work:

The Institute for Christian Leadership and Renewal, Salem, OR
This institute aids in the development of new clusters of Christian colleges.
1980-1982
Americans for International Aid and Adoption, Salem, OR
Escorting orphaned children from India and Korea to their new adopted homes in the U.S.
1982 - Present

Professional Affiliations:

Member: CASE (Council for the Advancement & Support of Education)
Member: Greater Salem Young Life Committee
Member: 1983 Campaign Cabinet, United Way of the Mid-Willmette Valley
Member: Yokefellows International
Former Member: City Club of Portland
Former Associate Director, Portland Rose Festival Association

RICHARD M. CHILDS *CHRONOLOGICAL / COMBINATION*

100 East Oak Road
Prospect Heights, IL 60070

708/555-0166

EXECUTIVE CHEF / EXECUTIVE SOUS CHEF

Career Highlights:
- More than 14 years of professional experience in the restaurant industry.
- Thorough working knowledge of regional American cuisine.
- Creative strength in Southwest, Caribbean and French cuisine.
- Effectively train, supervise, and motivate staff in all kitchen operations.

Professional Experience:

EXECUTIVE SOUS CHEF 1987-Present
The Purple Tiger (American/Regional), Barrington, IL
Responsible for entire kitchen operation including menu planning, daily specials, ordering and food costing.
Created seasonal menu to incorporate local ingredients in imaginative preparations.
- The Purple Tiger is a consistent leader in its regional market and has received critical acclaim from the Chicago print media.

EXECUTIVE CHEF 1986-1987
Scotland Yard Inn (Caribbean, American/Regional), Virgin Gorda, British Virgin Islands
Responsible for entire kitchen operation including menu planning, daily specials, ordering and food costing.
Positioned restaurant as successful culinary leader in the Virgin Islands.
- Created restaurant-brewed beers that sold successfully and increased bar revenue 25 percent
- Gained experience in handling a seasonal, tourist-impacted industry.

SOUS CHEF 1984-1986
Foodtypes, (Eclectic, American/Regional), Glencoe, IL
Planned menus and created daily specials.
Responsible for sautés, grilling, soups and sauces.
Handled cost-effective purchasing of all foods and equipment.
- Extensive education in the use of ethnic and regional American foodstuffs.

INDEPENDENT CONTRACTOR 1978-Present
Developed an independently owned and operated catering service, "Oasis", which features a wide variety of home-brewed beers.

ADVERTISING AND PUBLIC RELATIONS MANAGER 1978-1984
Employed as Copywriter in the advertising industry. Subsequently became Advertising Manager for Champion Auto Parts, Inc.
Developed communication, PR and business skills that have proven invaluable in the restaurant industry.

Education:
B.S. Degree, Advertising/Journalism, Arizona State University, Tempe, AZ

American Restaurant Association
Certified for completion of the Restaurant Management Program.

THOMAS F. MAJORS

319 Verde Drive
Arlington Heights, IL 60004

COMBINATION

708/555-5134

EXPERIENCE:
- Responsible driver with an accident-free record.
- Completion of Auto Mechanics and Technical courses.
- Bachelor of Science Degree in Education.
- Concentration in Math and Science.

EMPLOYMENT: RAPID PACKAGE SYSTEM　　　　10/86-1/89 and 6/89-1/90
Bedford, IL
Package Handler - (part-time)
Various duties included unloading trailers on dock.
Switched trailers for approximately three months.
Worked in fast-paced environment.

JERRY'S SHUTTLE SERVICE　　　　6/89-1/90
Crown Point, IN
Bus Driver - (part-time)
Transported college students to and from work and home.

MEMORY LANE CEMETERY　　　　5/88-8/88 and 6/89-8/89
Schererville, IN
Groundskeeper - (part-time)
Maintained grounds of cemetery property.

AMERICAN ARMATURE　　　　5/86-6/86
Blue Island, IL
Armature Rebuilder
Rebuilt starter motor armatures, including operating cutting lathe, sanding, buffing and testing for quality control.

VOLUNTEER SERVICES: Spanish Sunday School Teacher's Assistant.
Volunteer Bus Driver for college transportation department.

EDUCATION: HYLES-ANDERSON COLLEGE
Crown Point, IN
Bachelor of Science Degree in Secondary Education　　Graduated May, 1990

LINCOLN TECHNICAL INSTITUTE
Completed 20 weeks of course work in auto mechanics.

PERSONAL: Enjoy Scuba Diving, Hiking, Fishing and Intramural Football.

GRACE N. MICHAELS   *COMBINATION*

32275 Plum Creek Lane
Wheeling, IL 60090   708/555-7542

OBJECTIVE: A position where professional RN skills would be utilized.

EXPERIENCE:
- More than seven years in nursing, including six years in a psychiatric unit.

- Create and implement individual and group therapy techniques; plan and supervise counseling sessions for the milieu.

- Experience in primary nursing for trauma, med/surgical, pediatric, child/adolescent and psychiatric units.

- Working towards Master's Degree and Certification in Diabetic Teaching.

EMPLOYMENT:

Northwest Community Hospital, Arlington Heights, IL   10/90-Present
Staff RN
Responsible for primary nursing in a 39-bed med/surgical pediatric unit.
* Instruct new diabetics on symptom assessment and alleviation.
* Active member of the Shared Governance Council for this unit.

Denver General Hospital, Denver, CO   10/89-7/90
Staff LPN
Involved in successful team nursing, primarily in a trauma unit.
Floated occasionally to the adolescent psychiatric unit.

West Pines Psychiatric Hospital, Wheat Ridge, CO   1/89-1/90
Mental Health Counselor
In charge of the milieu on a daily basis.
Handled patient assessments and performed group and individual counseling.
* Assisted in the children's unit and floated to the adolescent unit as needed.

Children's Hospital, Denver, CO   12/88-1/90
Mental Health Counselor

Fort Logan Mental Health Center, Denver, CO   6/87-10/88
Mental Health Counselor
As counselor and milieu specialist, conducted one-on-one sessions with individual patients and maintained a safe, therapeutic environment.
Performed low and high-level interventions including RMA, TP, limit setting, seclusion and 4-6 pointing a patient.
Organized and managed role-playing groups, issue & rap sessions and young women's groups.
* Designed/structured milieu activities; acted as mediator between patient and case coordinator and charted daily/weekly patient progress.
* Supervised off-unit recreational therapy groups, as well as an evening special snack program.
* Earned Patient Appreciation Award.

GRACE N. MICHAELS

City and County of Denver, Denver, CO   9/84-8/87
Case Service Aide III
Performed one-on-one sessions with children having conduct disorders and restrained them when necessary.
Admitted children from birth to 12 years of age; documented their history and examined them for bruises and marks.
* Provided support for physically and sexually abused children through small groups and education.
* Designed and implemented structured play activities and craft projects.
* Conducted feelings/values clarification groups.
* Provided a nurturing, stimulating atmosphere for failure-to-thrive children.

The Baptist Home Association, Wheat Ridge, CO   9/84-11/84
Nurses' Aide
Attended to ADLs of elderly patients and performed colostomy care.
Provided positive reinforcement and a caring atmosphere.

VOLUNTEER EXPERIENCE:

Volunteers of America, Denver, CO   1986
Supervised activities at the Bannock Shelter for adolescent boys.

Channel 9 Health Fair, Denver, CO   4/87
Participant

EDUCATION:

Loretto Heights College, Denver, CO
B.S. Degree - Nursing   5/87
* Worked with the Denver Social Services Sex Abuse Team.
* Taught childhood safety and developmental stages to a new mother in her own home.
* Attended numerous seminars offered by Denver Social Services and the Fort Logan Mental Health Center:

- Milieu Management
- Borderline Personality
- Separation Anxiety
- O.T. Therapy
- Psychotropic Drugs
- Therapeutic Relationships
- Legal Restraints
- Failure to Thrive Children
- The Deaf Child and How To Communicate
- Sexual Abuse: Signs and Symptoms
- Plain Talk About Dealing with the Angry Child
- Play Therapy for the Sexually Abused Child
- Restraining and Physical Intervention

AWARDS & ACCOMPLISHMENTS:

* Alpha Chi National Honor Scholarship Society
* High Honors: Dean's List
* Loretto Heights College Scholarship
* Maintained 3.25/4.0 GPA while working at least 30 hours a week and raising four children.

PETER GABRIEL *COMBINATION*

4546 Hawkeye Drive
Wheaton, IL 60090   708/555-3215

OBJECTIVE: **Counseling**
A position where professional skills would be utilized.

EXPERIENCE:
- Experience in individual counseling, problem assessment and documentation, as well as the development and scheduling of group activities.

- Proven ability to communicate with juveniles from age 12, adult prison inmates, gang members and DCFS wards.

- Effective listener and counselor; provide active, ongoing support and guidance.

VOLUNTEER WORK: John Howard Association, Chicago, IL   1990-Present
Counselor
Directly involved in counseling prison inmates on personal problems and documenting their living conditions at numerous state correctional centers.

EMPLOYMENT: Cook County Temporary Juvenile Detention Center,
Chicago, IL   1990-Present
Children's Attendant
Responsible for counseling and maintaining law and order for 16 boys age 12-16.

First Western Mortgage Corporation, Wheeling   1987-1990
Customer Service Representative
Communicated directly with the clientele regarding account balances, payment due dates and customer complaints.
Operated a computer system for account tracking and updating.

MILITARY: U.S. Army, Sergeant - 2nd Armor Division   1983-1987
Effectively trained and supervised non-commissioned officers. This involved scheduling, accounting for soldiers, authorizing passes and dealing with A.W.O.L. soldiers.
* Counseled soldiers facing disciplinary actions and referred them to special organizations in cases of marriage or divorce.

EDUCATION: Harper College, Palatine, IL   1988-Present
Completion of courses in Criminal Justice, Sociology, Mathematics, Psychology and Racquetball.

Central Texas College, Killeen, TX   1986-1987
Courses included Public Speaking, College Algebra, Psychology, Public Speaking and English.

High School Graduate

HAROLD P. PATRICK   FUNCTIONAL

881 Payton Court
Northbrook, IL 60062
(708) 555-0182

FACILITY MANAGER/ENGINEER

EXPERIENCE

Management
- Work directly with inspectors, union officials, OSHA personnel, auditors and attorneys. Administer EEOC regulations and right-to-know legislation.
- Experience supervising union and non-English speaking employees.
- Supervise all phases of operation including production, inventory control and maintenance.
- Served as insurance risk manager. Obtained quotes, maintained policies, verified audits and filed workmen's compensation reports.
- Worked with general contractors, architects and engineers to develop plans for a $500,000 building construction and remodeling project.
- Served as on-site coordinator for all trades while still supervising plant operation.
- Instrumental in selection, design, installation and operation of a waste water pretreatment system. Represented company at Sanitary District hearings. Applied for local, state and federal regulatory permits. Filed subsequent reports.

Efficiency
- Designed and installed conveyor systems that eased work flow and increased production.
- Installed computer system that cut production time of weekly invoices in half. Redesigned the invoice to accommodate office, production, and delivery procedures more efficiently.
- Invented a pry-bar that cut manual demolition time by one-third.
- Extensive experience with high pressure boilers, three-phase electricity, pipe fitting, pneumatic and electric controls, pump and motor repair, and welding.
- Work with job shops to fabricate or repair obsolete and expensive parts to keep 30-year-old equipment operating.
- Skilled in the use of WordStar and Quattro for word processing and financial data compilation.

HAROLD P. PATRICK

EMPLOYMENT HISTORY

1989 - 1990   **Project Manager**, Autumn Cleaners
               Large retail facility with annual sales of $1.5 million.

1963 - 1989   **Plant Manager**, Perfect Uniform Rental Service
               Industrial laundry with annual sales of $3 million.

1970 - 1972   **SP-5**, U.S. Army (Vietnam).
               Honorably Discharged.

LICENSES

City of Chicago **Stationary Engineer's License**

EDUCATION

Bachelor of Science, Southern Illinois University, Carbondale, IL, 1968

CONTINUING EDUCATION

Studies: Robotics
            Stationary Engineering
            Computers
            Welding
            Machine Shop Math

RANDY L. REDMON   *COMBINATION*

920 Chestnut #515   Glenview, IL 60025   708/555-8769

OBJECTIVE: Property Management

PROFESSIONAL SUMMARY

- More than two years in successful property management, including full responsibility for lease negotiation, contractor scheduling, budget management and extensive commercial/residential customer relations.

- Staff hiring, training, and supervision; compile and present detailed status reports and analyze related expenditures.

- Experience in market research and the coordination of cost-effective advertising, marketing and promotional programs.

- Utilize WordPerfect and Skyline to produce resident and investor correspondence; organize billing and invoicing procedures to meet specific business needs.

EXPERIENCE

Underwriter's Management Corporation, Chicago, IL   4/88-8/90

Property Manager   9/88-8/90

Responsible for all promotional, leasing, and maintenance activities for a 17 story combined residential/commercial use building on Chicago's Gold Coast.

Supervised a staff of seven including maintenance personnel and doormen; conducted regular performance reviews of all employees.

Managed all budgets; screened and hired subcontractors and tradesmen; compiled and distributed lease expiration and weekly traffic/activity reports to all investors.

- Maintained 100 percent occupancy rate through effective advertising and sales presentations.
- Assisted in legal proceedings as needed for evictions and delinquent accounts.
- Promoted to this position from **Receptionist: 4/88-9/88**.

Superb Development, Deerfield, IL   3/85-4/88

Project Coordinator

Acted as liaison between buyers and construction contractors building customized, single family homes. Assisted in selecting options, prepared contracts and assured quality of completed work.

JEFFREY H. McGYVER *COMBINATION*

57 Weidner Road
Buffalo Grove, IL 60089 708/555-3086

OBJECTIVE: A Sales position in the incentive industry, where proven account management skills would be utilized.

EXPERIENCE:
- More than two years in professional incentive program sales, including key account prospecting, acquisition and management responsibilities.

- Conduct in-depth analyses of client's industry, distribution network, and sales force to create specialized, self-liquidating motivational programs based on incremental profits.

- Excellent ability to locate and develop profitable, personalized relationships with key corporate decision makers.

- Experience in comprehensive market research and the writing of custom sales brochures and literature.

EMPLOYMENT: **Account Executive** 7/88-Present
Arty Incentives, Niles, IL
Responsibilities include extensive cold calling, account prospecting and sales presentations to executive-level clientele throughout Chicagoland.
Industries include telecommunications, insurance, farm equipment and machinery, general industrial equipment and HVAC products.
Conduct field/library research and comprehensive interviews with potential clients, their employees, including dealers, distributors and their agents.
Demonstrated expertise in the facets of merchandising, travel, administration, recognition and communications/promotions.

- Personally generated $1.6 million in revenues since joining this firm.
- Achieved highest profit margin for 1990: 22.9 percent.

EDUCATION: **Bachelor of Business Administration** May, 1988
Concentration: Marketing
Pacific Lutheran University, Tacoma, WA

Internship:
Planned and conducted a detailed research of the frequent flyer program for Pacific Southwest Airlines/US Air. New policy was implemented for these airlines as a result of this analysis in 1988.

PERSONAL: Willing to travel or relocate.
Self-motivated and energetic, with professional communication skills.

NANCY A. GRAHAM *COMBINATION*

70 Kenneth Circle
Elgin, IL 60129   708/555-2258

OBJECTIVE: Continued career growth in the Food and Lodging industry.
Particular areas of interest include Accounting, Management, Marketing, and Regional or District Office Operations.

PROFILE:
- Proven ability to train and supervise up to 50 employees; experience as General Manager of two economy hotels.

- Trained in profit/loss balancing and long & short-term budget planning.

EXPERIENCE: HOLIDAY INNS OF AMERICA   10/89-Present
Prospect Heights, IL
General Manager
Effectively supervise 20 employees, including hiring and training.
Oversee front desk, maintenance, and housekeeping personnel.
Maintain accurate inventories and order all necessary supplies.
Bill corporate accounts and handle sales, including group bookings.

BLUE TIDE INNS   3/87-8/89
Shreveport, LA   9/88-8/89
General Manager
Responsible for hiring, training, and supervising up to 18 employees.
In charge of front desk operations, housekeeping staff and assistant manager.
Improved budget process and sales through effective balancing of P&L; maintained inventory and ordered supplies.

Dallas/Carrolton, TX   4/88-9/88
Assistant Manager
Accepted full responsibility for inventory, payroll and profit/loss of the operation.
Trained and supervised ten employees in all customer service and sales activities.

Downers Grove, IL   5/87-4/88
Assistant Manager
Similar duties to those described above with a staff of 23 employees.

Trainee   3/87-5/87

PONDEROSA STEAK HOUSE   10/86-3/87
Schaumburg, IL
Manager
Promoted to a new "turn-around" management team at this store plagued by poor performance. Responsibilities included supervision and scheduling of 35-55 employees; stock inventory and reorders, purchase of repair services, bill posting, labor hour calculation and P&L troubleshooting.

* Staff recruiting and training was a major part of this position, and the key to improved profits.
* Personally created recruiting programs and conducted presentations at high schools, trade shows and health departments.

* Planned and implemented training programs and evaluated worker progress.
* As a result of these actions, employee morale improved and turnover decreased. Quality control was upgraded and traffic volume increased.

PONDEROSA STEAK HOUSE   10/84-10/85
Elgin, IL
Assistant Manager
Similar duties as above while training.

SAGA CORPORATION
W.I.U., Northfield, IL   1982-1984
Cook's Helper/Key Student
Responsible for serving salads and beverages in this part-time position.

EDUCATION: WESTERN ILLINOIS UNIVERSITY, Macomb, IL
Bachelor of Science Degree in Food and Nutrition Graduated 5/84
Specialization: Food and Lodging   Minor: Business

Business subjects included marketing, management, personnel and accounting.
Utilized a Macintosh computer and WordPerfect 5.1.
Activities: Food Committee Representative, 1982.
Western Illinois Ski Club, 1980-1983
   Vice President 1982-1983
Earned Sanitation Certificate, State of Illinois, 1984

ADDITIONAL TRAINING: Earned Certificates from Blue Tide Inns for completion of:
Management Training Program, 1987
Motivating and Team Building, 1989
Coaching & Developing the Assistant Manager, 1989
Interaction Management Seminar, 1988
Hospitality Seminar, 1988

PERSONAL: Willing to travel or relocate; enjoy reading, bowling, darts and water/snow skiing.

PAUL A. MOCKI   *ENTRY-LEVEL COMBINATION*

8022 East Old Willow Road #11
Prospect Heights, IL 60070   708/555-9100

OBJECTIVE: A growth-oriented position with an environmentally conscious organization, where communication, organizational and managerial skills would be utilized.

EXPERIENCE:
- Proven abilities in report preparation, laboratory research, bookkeeping and general business administration.

- Familiar with IBM/DOS systems; utilize WordPerfect and Lotus 1-2-3; handle customer service and conduct speeches and presentations in a professional manner.

EDUCATION: St. Mary's College of Minnesota, Winona, MN
Bachelor of Arts Degree -- Environmental Biology   August, 1990
* **WAISE Scholarship Recipient, 1990**
* Completed an Undergraduate Thesis on Solid Waste Management. Examined waste management decisions affecting the environment. Conducted extensive research and interviewed state, city and county representatives.
  Analyzed the politics of environmental decision making and presented findings.
* Lab work included comprehensive studies of water chemistry.
* Created a detailed, hypothetical land use plan.
* Courses included hands-on experience in:

    - Ecology   - Limnology   - Ornithology
    - Botany   - Zoology   - Physics & Calculus
    - Chemistry   - Telemetry   - Taxonomy

EMPLOYMENT: Sybaris Inn, Wheeling, IL   June, 1990-Present
Front Desk Clerk / Night Auditor
In charge of all hotel activities during night shift -- including bookkeeping and direct customer service -- for this hotel with 136 rooms and a restaurant.
Work directly with vendors; process accounts receivable and cash receipts.
Supervise guest groups; handle check-ins/outs and assist the manager in all operations.

River Trail Nature Center, Northbrook, IL   Summer, 1989
Naturalist Aide
Acted as an information resource to the public and presented interpretative talks regarding nature and the Forest Preserve District.
Cared for Nature Center animals, assisted in construction projects and maintained nature center grounds and trails.

Prior Employment: McDonald's Restaurant, Mt. Prospect, IL   Summer, 1988
Crewperson -- provided efficient, quality service to all customers.
* Recognized as Crewperson of the Month, June, 1988

St Mary's College, Winona, MN   Summer, 1987
Maintenance Worker

1435 N.E. Sheridan Way Boca Raton, FL 33432	TERRA BEGGS	COMBINATION 407/555-8478

EXECUTIVE SECRETARY

EXPERIENCE:
- Proven abilities in virtually all secretarial and administrative activities, including full responsibility for meetings, travel plans and special events.

- Skilled in shorthand, dictaphone, typing and correspondence writing, as well as WordPerfect and DisplayWrite IV; familiar with Lotus 1-2-3 and all types of general office equipment.

- Experience in total office management in absence of senior-level personnel; enjoy multiple tasks in fast-paced business environments, with personal, yet professional communication skills.

EMPLOYMENT:

House Mortgage Group, Rosemont, IL   7/92-12/92
Administrative Assistant to the President
Responsible for a wide range of office functions including correspondence writing/distribution and professional telephone communications.
Organized travel itineraries and accommodations; purchased tickets, typed, filed and expedited messages and business schedules for the president.

Ant Hill Systems, Inc., Chicago, IL & Crawford, IN   9/87-5/92
Executive Secretary to the President & CEO
Organized a variety of functions for senior management of the corporate office and affiliates of this multi-divisional healthcare system.
Prioritized highly sensitive issues and events, including high-level meetings, calendars and business/personal travel plans.
Accurately typed all general and confidential correspondence.
* Promoted from: Executive Secretary to Chief Operating Officer & CFO; Executive Secretary to Vice President, Human Resources; Secretary to Corporate Director, Operations and Planning.

Anton's Union Station, Union, IL   4/86-9/87
Assistant Manager
Managed a 100-patron restaurant & lounge operation, including daily supervision and scheduling of wait staff.
Handled cost-effective purchasing of all food, beverages and supplies.

The Milwaukee Road, Chicago, IL   9/70-4/86
Administrative Assistant to the Vice President of Operations
Managed virtually all office functions and investigated freight damage claims with shippers and yard staff.
* Promoted from Secretary to Manager of Operations and Word Processing.

EDUCATION:
College of DuPage, Glen Ellyn, IL
Completed courses in office operations & computer systems.

GIUSEPPE L. MIRAND   COMBINATION

1751 Brewster Lane
Schaumburg, IL 60193   708/555-3174

OBJECTIVE: A position where professional Accounting skills would be utilized.

EXPERIENCE:
- More than 11 years combined experience in accounting, including full responsibility for department procedures, budgets and computer operations.

- Plan and conduct audits and variance analyses; process payrolls, personal & corporate taxes and maintain accurate inventories.

- Staff training and supervision in accounting activities and the use of Lotus 3.1 and Supercalc 5; familiar with full system conversions.

EMPLOYMENT:

Czarnowski Display Service, An exhibit set-up & service firm
Accounting Manager   Chicago, IL 12/90-Present
In charge of accurate, timely processing of accounts payable/receivable, payroll, insurance & union reports and sales/payroll tax returns.
Utilize Lotus 1-2-3 for job costing, account analysis and general ledger maintenance.
* Directly involved in converting an IBM System 34 to a Novell Network.
* Prepare monthly and annual financial statements.

SICPA Ink Systems, A manufacturing firm
Accounting Manager   Elk Grove, IL 1/88-9/90
Trained and supervised five employees in accounting activities.
Coordinated and prepared budgets; analyzed and interpreted forecasts, capital expenditures and financial data.
* Evaluated operational systems and procedures, as well as financial reporting methods on a regular basis.
* Analyzed cost variances and monitored inter-company transactions.
* Supervised a conversion using AS400 and Lotus 1-2-3.

Laventhol & Horwath, Public Accounting
Senior Accountant   Chicago, IL 6/82-12/87
Performed detailed financial audits of numerous businesses and recommended improvements in client's system procedures, documentation and internal controls.
Conducted reviews and compilations.
Prepared corporate and individual income tax returns, payroll and sales taxes.

U.S. Riley Corporation, A manufacturing firm
Cost Accountant   Skokie, IL 9/79-5/82
Assisted in budget forecasting; developed standard cost data and variance analyses.
Reviewed capital expenditures and coordinated/reconciled physical inventory.

EDUCATION: Letran College, Philippines
B.S. Degree: Accounting   1979

324 Bush Street	**WILLIAM DiNERO**	*COMBINATION*
Bartlett, IL 60103		708/555-1835

OBJECTIVE: A position utilizing extensive experience in software design and development.

EXPERIENCE:
- More than seven years combined experience in software and hardware development, including full responsibility for detailed system documentation and troubleshooting.

- Comprehensive experience with 6502 and 68000 Assembler, Turbo Assembler, Turbo C, Fortran, BASIC, Schema II+, Tango PCB and high-speed digital hardware.

EMPLOYMENT: Music Light, Inc. Bartlett, IL   1985-Present
Responsible for the set up and operation of this firm specializing in the design of state-of-the-art computerized lighting controllers.
Designed and developed a variety of products including hardware platforms and embedded, real-time software for controller systems.
Authored/created system documentation and a 200-page user's manual, complete with illustrations.
Negotiated contracts and worked successfully with financial and manufacturing representatives for system production and sales through an outside firm.

* Created 6502-based hardware platforms which use PLDs and EEPROMs. Captured schematics using Schema II+ and designed PCB art work with Tango Route on an IBM XT.
* Created a product simulator which enables a Turbo XT to read an industry standard serial data stream and reflect this information in a real-time graphics display. Utilized Turbo C and Turbo Assembler to develop a custom program which included high-speed drivers for serial communications and EGA graphics. This enabled the simulator to meet the requirements of a 250 KB data input rate and a 20 HZ screen refresh rate.

Emerson Electric Company, St. Louis, MO   1984-1985
Performed detailed software and hardware design for defense applications.

* Designed and developed embedded real-time 68000 assembly code used on a 68000-based hardware card which acted as an administrator for an image processing sub-system consisting of 10 dedicated hardware boards. The 68000 board also communicated with a ROLM military computer which acted as the administrator for the entire system, an advanced target cuing system to be used on U.S. M-1A1 tanks.
* Successfully designed and developed a video memory card which interfaced an RS 170 video output with a series of dedicated hardware cards used to incorporate various image processing algorithms.

EDUCATION: University of Illinois, Urbana-Champaign, IL   1984
B.S. Degree, Electrical Engineering -- Dean's List.
Admitted to Tau Beta Pi Engineering Honor Society

5188 C Robert Court
Bartlett, IL 60103

ROBERT E. CRAY

COMBINATION

708/555-4952

MECHANICS AND POWER PLANT MAINTENANCE/REPAIR

EXPERIENCE:
- More than 15 years as a mechanic, including full responsibility for powerplant re-building and maintenance to strict safety standards; Licensed Airframe and Powerplant Mechanic.

- Experience in quality control, project scheduling, work flow streamlining and detailed job inspection / documentation.

- Handle training, supervision and performance review in system repair and troubleshooting.

- Perform data entry and retrieval on computerized job control systems; compile and present written status reports in a professional manner.

- Skilled in the use of machine and hand tools ranging from grinders to micrometers.

EMPLOYMENT:

Aircraft Mechanic
USAF Reserves, O'Hare Airport, Chicago, IL   1979-Present
Responsible for daily inspection, testing, repair and troubleshooting of numerous aircraft including various tactical fighters and turbo-prop / airlift jets.
As Crew Chief, train and supervise up to eight mechanics in airframe and power plant maintenance, including lubrication, scheduled parts replacement and troubleshooting of hundreds of critical parts & systems. Duties include:

- Diagnostic Testing   - Installations
- Diagram/blueprint reading   - Fuel system repair
- Riveting and bolting   - Gear/flap maintenance

* Maintain top quality and safety standards on all work performed.
* Responsible for mobility equipment and regular calibration of testing devices.
* Utilize manufacturer's and FAA regulations for specifications to determine feasibility of component repair or replacement according to malfunction.
* Strong background in hydraulic systems, pneumatics and airframe controls.
* Maintenance duties include crankcase and screen cleaning, as well as brake rebuilding.
* Utilize a computer data base to track and update repair schedules as needed.

Tax Assessor
Wayne Township Assessors Ofc., Indianapolis, IN   4 Months, 1979
Responsible for the accuracy and quality of a high volume of reassessment data, used for accurate taxation of parcels and improvements.

Reviewer / Crew Supervisor
J.M. Cleminshaw Company, Cleveland, OH   1976-1978
Maintained the quality and integrity of computerized data used for processing area tax assessments.
Conducted real estate appraisals and trained new employees in all company procedures.

Jet Engine Mechanic
United States Air Force, Columbus Air Force Base, Columbus, MS   1968-1972
Involved in virtually all aspects of engine repair on aircraft which included J-57 (F-100) and J-85-5 (T-38) jet engines.
Assumed responsibility for maintenance schedules and assured prompt replacement of time-controlled components.

* Trained numerous section mechanics.
* Worked directly with the Engine Controller and reported to the Chief of Maintenance.
* Completed 11-months' service in Vietnam.

EDUCATION: Ball State University, Muncie, IN
B.S. Degree   1972-1976
Double Major: Business and Marketing
* Self-funded 80 percent of college costs

Additional / Ongoing Military Training

Completed courses which include:
Core Automated, Maintenance Computer Systems
Aircraft Maintenance Technology
Worker Supervising and OTJ Training

* Sustained Superior Performance: 1986, 1988, 1989 and 1990.

ELIZABETH A. LYNCH   *COMBINATION*

182 East Bailey Road #J
Naperville, IL 60565   708/555-7434

OBJECTIVE: A position where RN, Technical and Analytical skills would be utilized.

EXPERIENCE: ■   More than three years combined experience in oncology, surgical and cardiac units, including full responsibility for patient care and documentation.

■   Compile and present care plans and written reports with strong analytical skills; organize data on computerized systems; utilize charts, graphs and WordPerfect 5.1.

■   Plan and conduct staff and patient in-services in a professional manner; recognized for providing efficient, personalized patient care.

EMPLOYMENT: Hospital's Home Health Care, Aurora, IL   Pt. Time, 3/91-Present
Home Health Nurse
Provide effective in-home care for oncology patients.
Duties include the set-up of infusion pumps, drawing blood, monitoring morphine intake and regular tracking of patient progress.

NurseFinders, Aurora, IL   Pt. Time, 1/90-Present
Nurse
While attending college, provide professional care at a variety of hospitals.
Departments include surgical, orthopedic, cardiac and neurology.

Copley Hospital, Aurora, IL   5/87-1/90
Staff Nurse - Oncology and Hematology Departments
Responsible for 5 to 10 patients daily, including regular administration of chemotherapy and related I.V.s.
Dispensed whole blood, platelets, and cryoprecipitate; maintained access to central venus catheters.
*   Provided special care for radiation implant patients.
*   Planned and presented in-services for patients and staff; topics included dealing with side effects of radiation therapy, catheter maintenance and the setup of home infusion pumps.
*   Nominated by four different patients for the H.E.R.O Award.

EDUCATION: Kishwaukee College, Malta, IL   1987
Associate Degree - Nursing
*   Earned Scholarships from the Waterman Lion's Club and the 40:8 Society.

Aurora University, Aurora, IL   8/90-Present
Enrolled in courses towards a Bachelor Degree in Pre-Med/Health Science.

	PERRY PODGORNIAK	*COMBINATION*
310 Flagstaff Lane		
Hoffman Estates, IL 60194		708/555-2453

HVAC REPAIR AND MAINTENANCE

EXPERIENCE:
- Hands-on training in HVAC system troubleshooting, repair and maintenance: refrigeration, air conditioning, heating systems and electronics.

- Experience in direct customer service and efficient business operations; handle sales and problem solving in a professional manner.

- Skilled in price quoting, upselling, purchasing and order expediting with vendors; organize billing, shipping/receiving and general office functions.

EMPLOYMENT:

Z & Z Fasteners, Wood Dale, IL   10/89-Present
Inside Salesman
Handle extensive customer communications and the sale of virtually all types of fasteners, primarily to industrial accounts.
Determine specific needs of new and established customers on a daily basis, and suggest appropriate products to meet those needs.
Accurately quote prices and delivery times.
Track and process orders on the company computer terminal; utilize FAX machines, copiers and general office equipment.
* Promoted to this position from **Shipping Clerk**, with responsibility for billing, order filling, shipping/receiving and customer pickups. Utilized UPS and common carriers.

Minolta Corporation, Elk Grove Village, IL   10/84-7/89
Shipping Clerk
Responsible for order filling and shipping through various carriers.
Maintained accurate inventories and prepared bar codes for all merchandise entering and leaving the building.
Completed bills of lading and routed shipments to proper carriers and destinations.

EDUCATION:

Triton College, River Grove, IL   1/90-Present
Enrolled in the **A.A.S. Program** for Heating/Air Conditioning and Refrigeration Repair.
Successful completion of HVAC courses including:
* Refrigeration & Air Conditioning I & II, Applied Electricity/Refrigeration, Applied Electricity/Schematic Reading and Commercial Refrigeration.
* Completed Seminars through R.S.E.S.: Electronic Spark Ignition and Hydronics, and the American Standard Air Conditioning Tune Up Seminar.

W.R. Harper College, Palatine, IL   1/78-6/78
Completed 11 credit hours in Liberal Arts.

High School Graduate   6/77

	ANNIE GREENSPRINGS	*COMBINATION*
630 Point Drive		
Arlington Heights, IL 60004		708/555-9816

MARKETING / ADVERTISING

EXPERIENCE:
- More than seven years in creative sales, marketing and advertising coordination, including full project management responsibilities.

- Design and expedite large-scale, multi-media marketing and promotional programs in major markets; organize all aspects of writing, graphic arts and production for printed materials.

- Experience in account prospecting and acquisition; plan and implement sales proposals; proficient in Windows, WordPerfect, Lotus and Microsoft Word for Macintosh.

- Handle job costing, budget development and forecasting; assist in cost-effective vendor sourcing; determine and meet specific client needs.

- Train and supervise sales and creative staff at virtually all levels.

EMPLOYMENT: Purple Hills Country Club, Greenbrook, IL   3/92-Present
Marketing Coordinator
Assist the Food and Beverage Director in special projects, promotions and advertising for the F & B department, including the creative production and distribution of P.O.S. displays, newsletters, flyers, posters and direct mail pieces.

* Wrote, designed and printed an employee training and procedure manual.
* Work with banquet staff and coordinate food preparation and schedules for special events and parties.

SuperAds, Inc., Chicago, IL   3/88-1/92
Corporate Sales/Marketing Representative and Project Manager
Specialized in graphic display design: signage programs, barricades and window graphics.
Supervised up to 15 subcontractors in the coordination and production of large-scale, multi-media marketing programs.
Developed custom marketing strategies and media programs, involving design boards, copy writing/editing, keyline paste-up and transparencies.
Determined technical project specifications, i.e. cost, materials, placement, time and labor for the preparation of bids and proposals.
Handled scheduling of project fabrication and installation phases.
Utilized Lotus, WordPerfect, MS Word and Windows; gained experience in blueprint reading and interpretation.

* Top Sales Person for three years, with 90 percent repeat clients.
* Closed one of every three bids, with monthly sales up to $80,000.

* Designed and installed graphic displays for Sears Tower.
* Conducted research of current real estate projects and competitive products and services, with savings of up to 50 percent on specific projects.
* Determined and met specific client needs; conducted presentations and worked extensively with real estate developers, architects, designers and contractors in the use of graphic design for project promotion.

Japan Register Co. Northbrook, IL   8/85-3/88
Advertising Art / Marketing Coordinator
Supervised photographers and several projects simultaneously in the advertising department/print communications division.
Coordinated artwork and production for a 1,500 page annual catalog, direct mail flyers and brochures for hotels and resorts worldwide.
Provided direct creative input to vendors regarding artwork and copy for specific projects.

Assisted in photo styling, package design, layout, editing, proofreading and paste-up.
Specified typestyles, copy sizes, colors and placement of printed materials.
Supervised press checks, operated a stat camera and scaled transparencies.

* Maintained positive communications with purchasing staff and merchandise buyers.
* Acted as corporate representative at numerous industry trade shows.

EDUCATION: University of San Francisco, San Francisco, CA
B.A. Degree -- Art, Design Emphasis   1984
Minor: Art History

INTERNSHIPS: San Francisco Museum of Art   1984
Assistant Director: Coordinated all aspects of exhibits and programs.

University of San Diego   1982
Alumni Coordinator: Coordinated and planned alumni events; operated a computer for data entry related to former and future alumni.

Midco International   Summers, 1980-1981
Art Director / Assistant: Performed layout and keyline paste-up of brochures for a restaurant equipment company.

BLAME PETERS *COMBINATION*

1985 Longford Drive
Roselle, IL 60172

708/555-4059

OBJECTIVE: **Telecommunications Analyst**
A position offering the potential for supervision or management.

EXPERIENCE:
- More than nine years in telecommunications and four years in computer operations, including responsibility for multi-shift functions and complete hub planning and management.

- Experience in full system design, installation, analysis and troubleshooting for E-mail, file transfers, large data base networks and wide area networks.

- Hire, train and supervise technical staff in system repair and data base updating; determine & solve hardware, circuit and software problems.

- Well-versed in high-speed data links and all levels of multiplexing, as well as full documentation of network management systems and modems.

- Utilize and maintain synchronous/asynchronous transmissions over various networks; skilled in Xerox systems, CODEX 6040 multiplexers and the 9800 network management system; experience with a wide range of mainframes and peripherals.

EMPLOYMENT: Unocal Corporation, Chicago, IL 8/88-Present
Telecommunication Technician
Perform second-level troubleshooting and analysis for telecommunication systems handling large volumes of data from Amoco offices and refineries worldwide. Communicate with virtually all levels of Amoco personnel to maintain system viability for E-mail, file transfers and a major data base network.
* Successfully directed the installation of Amoco's first network management system for analog circuits, a CODEX 9800.
* Primarily utilize an SNA network-X.25, microwave networks and a T-1 backbone.

Xerox Corporation, Park Ridge and Des Plaines, IL 4/73-8/88
Technical Support Manager 2/85-8/88
Planned and implemented procedures for the support of 450 users; managed an entire equipment room for the Field Service Organization.
Directed two technical specialists and an information systems coordinator; conducted staff career counseling and performance reviews.
Handled troubleshooting of Honeywell and Raytheon terminals and controllers, as well as Codex modems and ATTIS DSUs; tested coax cables for continuity.
* Coordinated equipment moves and installs with end users and electricians; tracked and resolved circuit related problems.
* Installed and maintained a Xerox Ethernet system and managed an inventory of all related equipment and circuits.

* Ensured accurate documentation and operations procedures, as well as environmental stability.
* Attended monthly planning sessions with users and senior-level staff.

Operations Manager 3/83-2/85

Managed a three-shift batch processing and telecommunications operation, using a Xerox Sigma 6 mainframe with CP-V software, a multi-tape drive, disc drive and high speed printers.
Maintained a high level of user service on a base of three Honeywell level 6 computers using GCOS/TPS software.
Provided a technical interface with vendors for documentation, safety/security and tape library audits.
* Conducted staff training, career planning and performance reviews.
* Responsible for expense controls related to overtime and supplies.
* During installation of an HP 3000/68, coordinated operations training and developed operational guidelines to support the parts warehouse.
* Organized the shutdown and removal of computer room equipment at the end of batch operations.

Senior Computer Operator / Schedule Planner 2/79-3/83

Developed run-time schedules, technical support and daily monitoring of computer room activities for three shifts.
Performed JCL modifications, disc contention and batch processing analysis.
Updated documentation and schedules for critical tape transmissions and quality control.
* Analyzed - and developed the process for - enhancing batch processing through-put and minimized reruns.
* Earned the Xerox "Praise Award" for outstanding achievement.

Computer Operator Trainee / Computer Operator 4/73-2/79

Responsible for batch and telecommunications processing on three shifts.
* Consistently met critical transmission and report schedules and documented all hardware errors and operational problems.

EDUCATION: Amoco Corporation
Completed various company courses including: PCP Network Operations, CLI & Telematics Directory Structure, PCP Hardware Installation and Maintenance, Performance Management, ISDN Protocols and DR2D Radio Maintenance.

Xerox Attended the Management Studies Program.
AMI Completed *Supervisory Skills* and *Working With People*.

Oakton Community College courses included Human Behavior.
DePaul University Enrolled in the School for New Learning towards a B.A. in Telecommunications.

	DONALD E. TILAN	COMBINATION

1625 Arnold Avenue
Streamwood, IL 60107

708/555-5079

OBJECTIVE: Construction / Building Management

EXPERIENCE:
- Proven abilities in the management of virtually all building construction/upgrade activities from concept to completion.

- Handle full budget development and implementation; organize subcontractors and ensure cost-effective materials purchasing; negotiate labor and material contracts in a professional manner.

- Supervise quality control and adherence to specifications by architects, engineers, developers and tradesmen; work directly with local building officials; proficient in blueprint development/interpretation.

- Coordinate all aspects of projects including bid preparation/analysis for parking lots, landscaping, masonry, plumbing, H.V.A.C., electrical, fixtures and roofing.

EMPLOYMENT: Montgomery Ward & Co., Chicago, IL and locations nationwide   1971-7/91
Project Manager   1986-7/91
In charge of all construction operations and fixturing for numerous new and existing Ward stores throughout the U.S., with projects ranging up to $10 million. Responsible for all building construction, maintenance and repair expenditures. Analyze/troubleshoot problems and supervise activities; provide financial/status reports, as well as full documentation of labor, materials and project specifications. Write and present proposals for new retail store construction and the upgrading of existing buildings including:

1991 Projects in Illinois:
New Stores: St. Charles, $2.3 million; Crestwood, $1.5m.
Remodelings: Vernon Hills, $250k; Oak Brook, new entrances, $600k; Chicago Ridge, $550k.

Involved in specification review and proposal development for the following projects until approval of contract:
Merrillville, IN: $320k repaving; Orland Park, IL, $480k repaving; Saginaw, MI, $710k repaving; Toledo, OH, $514k repaving; Joliet, IL, $600k repaving; Cedar Rapids, IA, $640k repaving, Fairview Hts, IL, $550k reroofing; Des Moines, IA, $150k masonry restoration.

Project Administrator for the first 50 percent of construction of new stores in: Midland, MI, $1.7m; Rochester, MN, $2.5m; Marion, IL, $2.8m.

Responsible for the successful completion and cost-effectiveness for the following maintenance projects on retail stores, 1990:
St. Louis, MO, $250k masonry restoration; W. Lafayette, IN, $330k reroofing; Pontiac, MI, $486k reroofing; Schaumburg, IL, $980k reroofing.

Managed all aspects of construction for the following new stores, 1990:
Irondequoit, NY, $6.4m; Manchester, CT, $8.9m; Bay City, MI, $2m; Coon Rapids, MN, $1.5m; Bradley-Northfield, IL, $2.9m; Danville, IL, $1.6m; Countryside, IL, $1.7m; Moline, IL, $3.4m.

Project Manager for new stores in 1989:
Buffalo, NY, $3.3m; Ithaca, NY, $1.5m; N. Attleboro, MA, $9.5m; Kingston, NY, $3.3m; Kingston, MA, $1.9m.

Remodeling/improvement projects, 1989:
Saugus, MA, $470k new air conditioner & chiller; L. Grove, NY, $450k reroofing, masonry restoration & new entrances; New Brunswick, N.J., $990k reroofing; Hackensack, N.J., $173k reroofing; Merrillville, IN, $398k repaving; Warwick, RI, $700k reroofing; Albany, N.Y., $1.6m reroofing & masonry restoration.

Territorial Fixturing Superintendent 1983-1985

Directed the completion of up to $5m in store retrofit and fixturing projects, including all phases of merchandising.
Simultaneously coordinated up to 80 tradesmen and Ward personnel; ensured conformance to budgets and time parameters.
Supervised all union tradesmen including Installers, Fire Protection Staff, Mechanical Installers, Electricians, Carpenters, Painters and Carpet Installers.

- Maintained records for all monies and projects and approved additional work as required.
- Analyzed/approved competitive bids from numerous trades.
- Coordinated the installation of a concessions, including facilities for optical department, financial network, photo departments and beauty salons.
*** Excellent track record of completing major store fixturings in 1983, 1984 and 1985 on time and under budget.

Planning Supervisor 1981-1983
Reroofing and Masonry Restoration, Existing Wards Facilities.
Successfully managed up to $12 million/year in restoration projects, including researching new construction methods, products and specific job/quality criteria.
Performed inspections of established Ward units, evaluated problems and recommended corrective measures to store and warehouse management.
Assembled and prepared accurate cost estimates; developed formal write-ups and bidder's lists for company approval.

Chief Planner 1971-1981
A full range of sales support activities included drafting and the planning/remodeling of auto centers, service centers, convenience and distribution centers, credit centrals and catalog/telephone sales & stockrooms.
Supervised fixturing changes for merchandising trends through staff communications.

AMANDA HUSIAN   *COMBINATION*

P.O. Box 2793
Darien, IL 60559   708/555-5260

OBJECTIVE: **Art Gallery Representative**
A position which utilizes proven sales and creative art skills.

EXPERIENCE:
- Professional experience in curating and contributing original work to numerous Fine Art exhibitions in the Chicagoland area.

- Proven creative abilities in various art mediums, including monotypes, pastels, acrylic and oil painting.

- Acknowledged communication and customer relation skills in high-pressure situations; familiar with WordStar and Lotus 1-2-3.

EMPLOYMENT: **Cooler Concepts,** Westmont, IL   1/90-6/92
Receptionist / General Office facilitator
Responsible for direct client relations on a daily basis, which involves sales, scheduling inquiries and writing correspondence.
Performed agency advertising and promotion through direct mailings and telemarketing.
Updated and maintained client files on a PC with Wordstar.

* Increased total sales volume over two years by 20 percent.

Enchanted Forest Boutique, Westmont, IL   1/90-6/92
Sales Associate
Conducted sales presentations in a professional manner.
Managed and coordinated merchandise inventory and prepared semi-annual inventory reports using Lotus 1-2-3.
Trained new personnel in sales and the marketing of merchandise through in-store customer contact and advertising flyers.

College of DuPage Art Gallery, Glen Ellyn, IL   1987-1989
Gallery Assistant
Assisted in curating major art shows on-campus.
Ensured prompt delivery, layout and installation of artwork.
Provided receptionist services and answered telephone inquiries during art shows and regular viewing hours.

* Coordinated art show schedules and original advertising distribution.

Jemster Gallery, Westchester, IL   Summer, 1988
Receptionist / General Office Facilitator
Responsible for the creative installation of new artwork.
Maintained client files and purchase records using a PC and Lotus 1-2-3.

ART SHOWS:

Columbia College, Chicago, IL   5/92
Curated Senior Art Show, including selection, organization and installation of 15 pieces.

Columbia College, Chicago, IL   5/92
One original acrylic painting on display.

NO EXIT Cafe and Gallery, Chicago, IL   4/92
Curated a personal art show with eight pieces, including paintings and monotypes.

River North Cafe, Chicago, IL   2/92
Contributed three monotypes to a group art show.

Avalon, Chicago, IL   2/91
Participated in a group art show with seven other artists and contributed mixed media pieces.

Diva Cafe, Chicago, IL   12/90-2/91
Curated a personal art show with 12 pieces on display, including drawings and acrylic paintings.

Columbia College, Chicago, IL   6/90
Participated in a student art show with two paintings.

College of DuPage, Glen Ellyn, IL   6/89
Participated in a student art show with one pastel.

College of DuPage Gallery, Glen Ellyn, IL   1987
Displayed a drawing and a photograph in a student art show.

EDUCATION:

Columbia College, Chicago, IL   1990-1992
B.A. Degree, Fine Arts

*   Maintained a full course load while working 25 hours a week.

College of DuPage, Glen Ellyn, IL   1986-1989
Completed course work toward Fine Arts degree.

JACQUELINE T. BARRET *COMBINATION*

1101 Bar Harbour #612
Schaumburg, IL 60193
708/555-6306

OBJECTIVE:	**Travel Agent** A position utilizing proven abilities in the travel industry.
EXPERIENCE:	▪ More than ten years in customer and technical services with several airlines. ▪ Experience in full travel expediting: ticketing, baggage supervision, pilot and aircraft scheduling and priority shipping; skilled in SABRE and SONIC reservation systems. ▪ Train and supervise personnel in company procedures, customer relations and problem solving in high-pressure situations.

EMPLOYMENT:

Delta Airlines, Chicago, IL 1989-Present
Passenger Service Agent
In charge of a full range of baggage services including investigation, tracing and reporting of lost or damaged items, as well as the processing of financial settlements.
Handle daily preparation of written reports and data entry/retrieval using SABRE.
Manage five employees as night supervisor and facilitate package routing.
*   Completed extensive training in Customer Relations.

British Airways, Chicago, IL 1985-1989
Customer Service Representative / Trainer
Responsible for all aspects of ticketing including check-ins, boarding/gate operations and transaction reporting.
Trained new employees in all areas of customer relations at corporate class sites.
*   Gained a working knowledge of SABRE and SONIC reservation systems.

Dubuque Greyhound Park, Dubuque, IA 1985-1986
Customer Service Agent / Financial Clerk
Assisted in daily reporting, data entry/retrieval and general ledger preparation.

American Central Airlines, Dubuque, IA 1982-1984
Customer Service Agent / Flight Controller
Handled all areas of customer relations, including ticketing, baggage investigation and claim settlement.
Coordinated crew and aircraft scheduling and maintenance; assisted in payroll processing and disbursement.

EDUCATION:

McConnell School - "20" Course, Minneapolis, MN 1982
Trained in airline travel procedures.

Northeast Iowa Technical Institute, Dubuque, IA 1981
Certified as Activity Coordinator.

	WILLIAM A. BRYERS, C.P.A.	COMBINATION
136 North Robinson		
Palatine, IL 60067		708/555-9538

CORPORATE CONTROLLER / MANAGER

EXPERIENCE:
- Proven abilities in accounting system design and management, including responsibility for staff coordination, financial reporting, audits and reviews.

- Experience with Lotus 1-2-3 and various general ledger packages, spreadsheet development and data compilation; handle all aspects of federal and state tax planning and preparation for large and small corporations.

- Train and supervise accounting staff in full ledger maintenance, billing, AP/AR and payroll procedures.

EMPLOYMENT:

<u>Astaire & Rogers, CPAs,</u> Chicago, IL   8/87-6/92
Supervisor
Responsible for up to six certified audits and numerous reviews and/or compilations at a wide range of companies on an annual basis.
Trained and supervised up to three professionals per project; determined and met specific client needs for complete ledger maintenance and reporting.
Recommended improvements to client systems and procedures to ensure strong internal controls.
Processed/reviewed federal and state individual and corporate tax returns.
* Manage complete accounting projects for firms with up to $277 million in annual sales.
* Maintain an up-to-date knowledge of current federal and state tax codes.

<u>Kargol & Salty, CPAs,</u> Oak Brook, IL   11/85-7/87
Certified Public Accountant
Performed accounting services for tax returns and real estate partnerships.
Distributed K-1s and updated/reported journal entries of year-end activity.
Prepared projections and forecasts for rental properties.

<u>Singer & Rogers, CPAs,</u> Chicago, IL   11/81-11/85
Senior Accountant
Handled all public accounting duties at numerous companies, including all federal and state tax preparation.

<u>Duey, Chetham & Howe CPAs,</u> Chicago, IL   12/79-10/81
Junior Accountant
Responsibilities included write-up work, assisting on audits and tax preparation.

EDUCATION:

<u>DePaul University,</u> School of Commerce, Chicago, IL   Graduated 1979
B.S. Degree -- Accounting Major   *Dean's List

<u>Wright Jr. College,</u> Chicago, IL   Graduated 1976
A.S. Degree -- Graduated with Honors

RUSSELL W. BIRD, JR. COMBINATION

4482 Aster Dr. #223
Schaumburg, IL 60173   708/555-8104

MACHINIST

EXPERIENCE:
- Proven abilities in production, supervision and quality control; thorough knowledge of Cincinnati and Mazak machine centers.

- Skilled in Computerized Numerical Control, SPC inspection and blueprint reading; utilize precision hand tools and measuring instruments.

- Familiar with engineering designs and product theory; interface with production, management and engineering staff at all levels of experience.

EMPLOYMENT: Super Tech Mold, Rolling Meadows, IL 1990-Present
Tool Machinist
Responsible for machine operations and quality assurance in the production of mold bases and plastic components.
Interface with CNC programmers and participate in SPC efforts.
Work directly with engineers and provide input regarding machinery and practical equipment applications.

* Leader of the Safety Board Committee; planned and implemented numerous plant safety procedures.

Teledyne Public, Cleveland, OH 1978-1990
Lead Machinist
Supervised and scheduled up to 12 employees in the precision manufacture of hydraulic and pneumatic valves.
Oversaw the CNC department and coordinated SPC quality assurance inspections.
Participated in production planning with senior-level personnel.

* Consistently met or exceeded the highest standards of quality for a demanding customer base.
* Completed company sponsored training in:

  - Quality Control and SPC
  - Blueprint Reading

EDUCATION: University of Akron, Akron, OH
Completed numerous courses toward a B.S. in Manufacturing Technology.
Current status: Junior.

FELICIA A. BURTON   COMBINATION

904 St. Clair Lane
Hanover Park, IL 60103   708/555-5057

OBJECTIVE:	**Counseling:** A position where professional communication skills would be of value.
EXPERIENCE:	■ Trained in the assessment of drug/alcohol dependencies, abnormal psychology and the tracking of individual progress. ■ Familiar with overall needs assessment and group/individual counseling. ■ Experience in teaching psychology and sociology; plan and conduct written and oral presentations in a professional manner. ■ Knowledge of WordPerfect and PC computer functions.
EDUCATION:	Eastern Illinois University, Charleston, IL **B.A. Degree -- Psychology** Graduated 5/91 **High School Teacher Certification** Performed 12 weeks of High School Student Teaching, including class planning/presentation and student supervision. Taught Psychology and Sociology to Juniors and Seniors at South Vigo High School, Terre Haute, IN. Personally tutored a Junior High School Student in History and various subjects. Courses included the study of Child Psychology, Adolescent & Abnormal Psychology, Mental Hygiene, The Exceptional Child and Teacher Preparation. Gained an excellent knowledge of drug/alcohol dependency assessment, fetal alcoholic syndrome, cocaine and drug-related problems and juvenile delinquency. * Activities/Memberships included: Alpha Sigma Alpha Sorority, Intramural Chairperson, Greek Week Chairperson for Two Terms, Psychology Club Member. * Self-funded 50 percent of college costs through employment at:
EMPLOYMENT:	**Customer Service Representative** 5/91-Present Zanies Comedy Club, Mt. Prospect, IL Handle customer communications and problem-solving on a part-time basis. **Lifeguard** Summers, 1987-1992 Dillon Recreation, Glendale Heights, IL Responsible for pool safety and communicating with patrons in a professional, yet personalized manner.

491 Foxboro Court
Streamwood, IL 60107

RONALD W. CAMPBELL

COMBINATION

708/555-0792

PHARMACEUTICAL / MEDICAL SUPPLY SALES

EXPERIENCE:
- More than five years in medical product sales, marketing and strategic planning, including full responsibility for account prospecting and management.

- Plan and conduct detailed product presentations for medical staff at all levels of experience; excellent knowledge of cardiovascular and antibiotic medications; skilled in new product introduction and marketing.

- Experience with hospital formularies; handle pricing, negotiations and all aspects of contract administration.

EMPLOYMENT:

<u>Searle Pharmaceutical,</u> Spring House, PA 1/87-Present
Sales Representative 4/89-Present
Responsible for selling various types of pharmaceuticals to hospital & office based physicians and pharmacies in a Chicagoland territory.
Plan and conduct detailed product presentations, following full product research.
Manage more than 300 accounts including six hospitals, three of which are teaching hospitals.
Responsible for all aspects of product distribution and account tracking on a PC; compile & present reports on product samples, inventories and account activity.
Handle full account troubleshooting and timely call-backs.

* Plan and conduct Continuing Medical Education (CME) accredited in-service programs for all types of medical personnel.
* Personally acquired two teaching hospital accounts.
* Contender for Stratosphere award, given for the highest market shares and change in share on promoted products within each region, 1990.
* Earned Regional Sales Award for top district sales in the region, 1989.

Corporate Representative 1/87-4/89
* Earned Sales Training Achievement Award (S.T.A.R.) for outstanding first year performance, including proficiency in product lines, sales skills, territory management and sales performance.

<u>Sherwin Williams Company,</u> Cleveland, OH 2/84-1/87
Manager
Performed marketing and sales to wholesale accounts.
Hired, trained and supervised sales personnel; processed credits and collections.
Promoted to this position from Operations Manager with a crew of 14.
Responsible for billing, inventory control, credit and store operations.

EDUCATION:
<u>University of Illinois at Chicago, IL</u>
Bachelor of Arts Degree -- Economics 8/83

	LINDA DAVESTER	*COMBINATION*
2406 Grant Drive		
Carpentersville, IL 60110		708/555-3597

CREDIT / COLLECTIONS REPRESENTATIVE

EXPERIENCE:
- More than ten years in credit/collection operations and loan review, including full responsibility for payment plans, rate negotiations and customer service.

- Determine credit limits and update & maintain client accounts on computer systems; familiar with Lotus 1-2-3, CDI software and the AT&T 705.

- Experience in training and supervising staff in professional credit and collection operations: credit checks, transaction processing & reporting and currency conversions.

EMPLOYMENT: Quickie Transportation Services, Wood Dale, IL   4/90-Present
Accounts Receivable Supervisor
Responsible for collections, credit policies, customer service and hundreds of accounts for this air freight transportation service.
Assist in supervising up to 16 employees in journal entries and compiling/presenting monthly status reports.
Work directly with branch office managers to resolve accounting issues and problems.
* Work extensively with "hard core" collections on a regular basis.
* Distribute cash on customer accounts and mediate disputed accounts.
* Prepare daily bank deposits and report directly to management.

Moon Electric Corporation, Crystal Lake, IL   3/87-8/89
Credit and Collections Specialist--
International Operations Division   3/89-8/89
Updated, maintained and distributed customer accounts on a daily basis, including the processing of incoming receivables for the international division.
Initiated and performed credit checks; established credit histories and authorized tracing of overdue drafts and/or letters of credit.
* Monitored day-to-day exchange rates for foreign currency conversions.
* Calculated percentages of commissions paid to distributors.
* Compiled and presented monthly statements of pre-existing distributors and customers for their reviews.
* Promoted to this position from **Administrative Secretary** and **Commission Administrator.**

The Quaker Oats Company / Stuart Laboratories, Barrington, IL   8/82-12/85
Serial Publication and Information Librarian

EDUCATION: Central YMCA Community College
Major: Business Administration; Career Major: Business Law

MARK L. AVON   *COMBINATION*

152 Parkview Circle East
Hoffman Estates, IL 60195   708/555-9352

OBJECTIVE: **Quality Assurance Engineering**
                   A position where proven technical skills would be utilized.

EXPERIENCE: ■ More than three years in quality assurance, including responsibility for specifications writing, product troubleshooting and corrective action.

                   ■ Experience in statistical analysis, SPC and documentation of specs and tolerances; organize suppliers and production staff at all levels of experience.

                   ■ Handle customer relations, quality surveys and internal procedure audits in a professional manner.

                   ■ Skilled in Lotus 1-2-3, Graphwriter, TimeLine, Multimate and the Crosby statistical process control program.

EMPLOYMENT: Ralph Crane, Inc., Morton Grove, IL   1/90-Present
                   Quality Assurance Engineer
                   Responsible for inspection and quality control procedures for this leading manufacturer of mechanical pump seals.
                   Quality Assurance Team Member, participating in a high-volume, engineered seal task force in the Appliance Seal and other high-volume, engineered seal Divisions.

                   Work directly with production staff and management for prompt discovery and correction of product defects.
                   Address causes of problems and provide corrective action and responses for customers.
                   Plan and conduct customer audits of plant operations; prepare and administer quality surveys on a regular basis.
                   Utilized X bar and R chart information to complete Cpk quarterly reports for the Ford Climate Control Division.

                   * Team Leader for the Quest Team, comprised of cross-functional departments and identifying/resolving problems related to scrap, rework and throughput.
                   * Analyze and improve internal procedures while involving shop workers in the decision-making process.
                   * Assembled statistical information for new part approval, in compliance with General Motors' "Targets For Excellence."
                   * Fulfilled corrective action responses for the GM Problem Reporting and Resolution Program.
                   * Designed and implemented a computerized program to record and analyze rejection information.
                   * Established a Material Evaluation Board for reviewing in-process rejections.

Engineering Laboratory Technician 7/89-1/90
Analyzed automotive seals for various failure modes and summarized results into technical reports for department heads.
Instrumentation experience included operation of a Sheffield Indicorder and a Talysurf model 10.

Specification Writer 10/88-7/89
Structured bills of materials in an AMAPS manufacturing system using information from blueprints and mainframe computer programs.

Anmark Publishing Company, Inc., Chicago, IL 9/87-10/88 and 9/86-4/87
Customer Service / Sales
Responsible for computerized data entry, circulation fulfillment and direct mail promotions.
Handled subscription sales and a variety of office duties.

Premier Industrial Corp., Kent Industries Division, Cleveland, OH 4/87-9/87
Sales Representative
Opened and serviced new accounts throughout the Chicagoland area.

EDUCATION: Keller Graduate School of Management, Chicago, IL
MBA Degree: Expected Graduation, 5/93

Marquette University, Milwaukee, WI
B.S. Degree: Industrial Engineering Graduated 5/86

Project Experience:
Developed and designed a new dental hygienist chair and redesigned a security ID checking station at the Helfaer University Recreation Center.

PROFESSIONAL MEMBERSHIP: Member of the Institute of Industrial Engineers.

PERSONAL: Enjoy Tennis, Physical Fitness, Camping and Working with PCs.

RALPH PREWICK   *COMBINATION*

720 North Opal Avenue
Norridge, IL 60656   708/555-2234

OBJECTIVE: **CAD / CAM: DESIGN ENGINEERING**
                     A position where proven skills in state-of-the-art systems would be utilized.

EXPERIENCE: ■   More than five years in virtually all aspects of product design, development, production and inspection on CAD/CAM systems.

                     ■   Trained in 3-D/finite element analysis and solids modeling; skilled in IBM CADAM, BRAVO and CAD-PAK systems.

                     ■   Experience in staff training and supervision in 2-D & 3-D design and drafting; assign/organize work and interface with technical staff and engineers in a professional manner.

EMPLOYMENT: Bluebird Hannifin Corp., Cylinder Division, Des Plaines, IL   1987-Present
                     Design Engineer, CAD/CAM Systems
                     Perform product design and development for this major manufacturer of cylinders, pistons, rods and all types of hydraulic and pneumatic equipment.
                     Train and supervise up to five employees.
                     Responsible for work scheduling, assignments and special projects.
                     Assist in all development functions for parts and finished products.

                     *   Work extensively with R&D personnel for new CAD/CAM designs.

                     William Rainey Harper College, Palatine, IL   1985-1987
                     Teacher's Assistant
                     Instructed students in drafting and design techniques.
                     Performed CAD-PAK 2-D drafting, BRAVO 2 & 3-D design, drafting, solids modeling and finite element analysis.
                     Tracked individual student performance; administered tests and answered technical questions.

EDUCATION: Purdue University, Calumet, IN   Expected Graduation, 1993
                     B.S. Degree -- Mechanical Engineering

                     William Rainey Harper College, Palatine, IL
                     A.S. Degree -- Pre-Engineering   Graduated 1987
                     *   Completed extensive training in CADAM, BRAVO and CAD-PAK systems.

COREY J. APPLE   *FUNCTIONAL/COMBINATION*

124 N. Joe Court
Addison, IL 60101   708/555-1260

OBJECTIVE: Pilot / Aircraft Mechanic
A position where solid flying skills and/or mechanical expertise would be utilized.

EXPERIENCE:
- Proven abilities in flying instruction; experienced with the Cessna 150, 152, 172, 172RG, Piper Warrior, Piper Aztec and Turbo Arrow.

- Licensed as Private Pilot, single and multi-engine land/instrument planes, Commercial Pilot, Airframe Mechanic, Powerplant Mechanic and Certified Flight Instructor.

- Skilled in a variety of shop equipment, as well as:

    -- Fiberglass & bonded honey comb repair
    -- Weighing & balancing of control surfaces
    -- Removal & replacement of skin panels & aircraft fasteners
    -- Manufacture and testing of control cables
    -- Comprehensive modification of aircraft structures
    -- Corrosion control and aircraft painting
    -- Power shears, band saws and the Conrac Synchrobender
    -- Erco sheet metal formers and the Di-Arco turret punch
    -- Hand and power rollers, belt sanders, drill presses, lathes & mills

EDUCATION: Southern Illinois University, Carbondale, IL
Bachelor of Science Degree -- Aviation Management   12/92
Associate Degree -- Aviation Maintenance   8/92
Associate Degree -- Applied Sciences   8/90

*   Overall GPA: 3.0/4.0

EMPLOYMENT: Self-funded college costs through employment at:

Mallard Construction Company, Bloomingdale, IL
Apprentice   Summers/Breaks, 1990-Present
Responsible for electrical, plumbing and carpentry work on office buildings, townhomes, single family homes and warehouses.

Aaron's Office Furniture Warehouse, Itasca, IL   Summers, 1988-1989
Forklift Driver / Order Puller

United Parcel Service, Addison, IL   1/86-7/87
Customer Service Representative
Performed shipping/receiving and truck loading & unloading on a daily basis.

JOSEPH NIECE *COMBINATION*

561 Washington Street
Elmhurst, IL 60126

708/555-6114

OBJECTIVE:	**Printing:** A position where extensive skills would be utilized.
EXPERIENCE:	▪ Proven abilities in virtually all aspects of printing, including full responsibility for press configuration, setup and teardown.
	▪ Hire, train and supervise press workers in makeready and quality control; work closely with customers in full project troubleshooting.
	▪ Handle color matching, registration and full press maintenance; experience with 4, 5, and 6-Color web presses, 17" to 38":

-- Harris M-1000 4-color web & sheeter *and* 6-color web with sheeter, double former folder and combination folder.
-- Harris M-110 4-color web with in-line finishing and sheeter
-- Hantsho 4-color web with in-line finishing & sheeter and 2-color w/sheeter
-- Didde Glaser 4-color web with in-line finishing and sheeter
-- Baker Perkins C-14 4-color web with in-line finishing and sheeter

EMPLOYMENT: Redmaster Rice, Elk Grove Village, IL   7/88-12/91
Pressman
Handled a wide range of printing projects on the Harris 6-color press, including direct customer service and problem solving on a daily basis.
Trained and supervised one pressman and two feeders in all operations.

Web Tech, Wheeling, IL   1983-1988
Foreman
Responsible for operation of seven presses, with sheeter and in-line finishing.
Worked closely with all customers and promptly resolved problems with quality and turnaround time.
*   Handled final approval of color quality.
*   Trained and supervised up to 40 employees.

Continental Web Company, Itasca, IL   1982-1983
Pressman
Duties included full makeready, color and register setup.
Communicated daily with customers regarding special projects and quality control.

Wessel Printing Co., Elk Grove Village, IL   1973-1982
First Pressman and Feeder

EDUCATION: High School Graduate

MILITARY: U.S. Army Veteran

JAMES T. RISE   *COMBINATION*

138 S. Commonwealth Avenue
Elgin, IL 60123   708/555-4478

OBJECTIVE: **Mortgage Banking Management**
A position where executive-level skills would be utilized.

EXPERIENCE:
- More than eight years in mortgage banking and management, including full responsibility for department operations.

- Hire, train and supervise staff in the monitoring of portfolio and inventory REOs, foreclosures and bankruptcies on computer systems.

- Coordinate all related documentation and services with attorneys, trustees and investors.

- Ensure timely filing of foreclosure claims with the FHA/VA and PMI, as well as compliance with FREDDIE MAC, FNMA and private investors.

EMPLOYMENT: Dove & Crow Mortgage, Inc., Schaumburg, IL   2/84-5/92
Assistant Vice President - Mortgage Disposition   12/90-5/92
Responsible for eight employees and all MD department operations, including customer service and the monitoring of up to 500 bankruptcies and 350 loans in the foreclosure and claims areas.
Ensure delivery of default letters; review new filings for possible cramdown characteristics.
Work with attorneys and agencies listed above for prompt, efficient service.
Reviewed all monthly status reports for accuracy.

* Direct staff and attorneys in the determination and resolution of specific problems.
* Plan and implement strategies for loss reduction and professional customer service.
* Promoted to this position from:

Assistant Vice President, Collections
Managed collection procedures for a portfolio of 50,000 loans, with an emphasis on FHA/VA loans.
Hired, trained and supervised more than 15 employees in all operations and conducted their performance reviews.
Analyzed/reviewed all files prior to submission to the foreclosure review board.
Ensured compliance with FREDDIE MAC, FNMA and private investor requirements; maintained accuracy of monthly reports sent to all investors.

Assistant Manager, Escrow Department
Hired, trained and managed 20 employees in hazard insurance claim processing.
Consistently reviewed and improved procedures & operations.

Special Task Force: Assistant to the President
Responsible for troubleshooting of receivables, MIP open items and PMI open items.

Ludwig Dairy Corporation, Elgin, IL   1979-1984
Machine Operator
Operated plastic injection molding and filling machines in a safe, cost-effective manner.

Car-Mon Products, Elgin, IL   1976-1979
Plant Manager
In charge of all plant operations and the training and supervision of up to 15 employees.
Responsible for purchasing, inventory control, shipping and distribution.

EDUCATION: The Mortgage Banking Association
Certificate for completion of various courses

T. Frank Hardesty Seminar:
The Art of Managing Collections

Saint Edwards High School, Elgin, IL   Graduated 1963

2653 Catalpa Lane	STEVEN B. TIRED	COMBINATION
Bartlett, IL 60103		708/555-0798

OBJECTIVE: Solid / Hazardous Waste Management
A position where hands-on training would be utilized.

EXPERIENCE:
- Proven abilities in research and material/cost estimating; trained in biomonitoring system design and analysis; familiar with RCRA and CERCLA legislation.

- Handle written & oral communications in a professional manner; strong aptitude for learning technical systems and procedures.

- Familiar with Lotus 1-2-3 and Quattro for spreadsheets, as well as WordPerfect 5.1.

EMPLOYMENT:

<u>Village of Elgin,</u> Elgin, IL   Summer, 1991
Internship
Assisted in material and cost estimating for several village projects.
Responsible for collecting measurements of sidewalks and streets, and updating all documentation.
Involved in setting slopes at construction sites.
Collected data and handled plan reviews, as well as a variety of field work.
Communicated with city residents regarding problems and complaints.

<u>American Flange,</u> Carol Stream, IL   Summers
Materials Handler

<u>Builders Square</u> and <u>Walgreens</u>   School Breaks & Summers
Cashier / Customer Service Representative

EDUCATION:

University of Illinois at Urbana-Champaign, IL
Bachelor of Science Degree   May, 1992
Major: Civil Engineering   **Concentration: Environmental Engineering**
* Major GPA: 4.3/5.0
* Self-funded 100 percent of college costs.

* Class projects included extensive research and the writing of a major report on surface drainage of an urban creek.
* Key courses included:
Wastewater Management
Air & Water Quality Control
Solid and Hazardous Waste Management
Biomonitoring

211 Walker
Streamwood, IL 60107

JEROME WUDYKA

COMBINATION

708/555-4894

OBJECTIVE:	**Programmer / System Analyst** A position in a PC environment, where diverse technical skills would be utilized.
EXPERIENCE:	■ Proven abilities in application programming, system design and support for a variety of businesses, in a data processing service bureau. ■ Fluent in IBM assembler (ALC); familiar with COBOL, RPG, DOS/VS and DOS/VSE. ■ Experience with hardware including the ES 9000, the 4300 series, S/370 model 135, S/360 models 30 & 40 and the Nixdorf system 680. ■ Skilled in manual/computer conversions, as well as staff supervision and the writing of numerous accounting applications.

EMPLOYMENT: <u>NASA Data Corporation,</u> Park Ridge, IL   1965-4/92
Production Support Analyst   1990-4/92
Responsible for the design, writing and maintenance of all programs for numerous businesses, including troubleshooting and debugging.
Applications included accounts payable/receivable, payroll, order entry, inventory control, sales analysis, cost analysis "Fix It" and various conversion programs.
Programmed and maintained the AT&T system 75 telephone system.
Performed troubleshooting of programs distributed by the national support center; handled program changes, adds & deletions.

   *   Utilized all hardware and languages listed above, as well as the IBM 1401 and CDC Omega 480.
   *   Produced over 350 programs on IBM systems.
   *   Promoted to this position from:

Associate Project Analyst
Performed system design and handled extensive customer relations and problem solving in a professional manner.

Programmer Analyst
Designed and wrote a wide range of application programs.

Programmer
Utilized Autocoder, IBM Assembler and COBOL for program production.

EDUCATION: <u>Roosevelt University,</u> Chicago, IL   1971
Bachelor General Studies Degree -- Computer Science

EDWARD SLICK   COMBINATION

5N376 Fairway Lane
Itasca, IL 60143   708/555-9052

EXPERIENCE:
- Comprehensive technical writing skills developed through in-depth product research and system documentation, including full responsibility for user manuals and reports.

- Experience in civilian and military projects, including specification development, test reporting and variance analyses.

- Work directly with engineers and designers for prompt updating of all written materials, including instructional, operational & service manuals.

- Utilize WordPerfect, WordStar, PageMaker and Ventura Publisher.

EMPLOYMENT: Sony Electronics Corporation, Glenview, IL   1990-1/92
Senior Technical Writer
Performed product research and technical/non-technical writing of operating manuals and documentation, primarily for TVs, VCRs and Camcorders.
Handled writing, data compilation, layout and design of materials using desktop publishing software listed above.
Worked extensively with product designers and engineers, as well as staff in purchasing and marketing departments.
Provided full technical support and liaison functions with Sony distributors and service technicians.
Consistently transformed incomplete or confusing technical/instructional material into accurate, usable information by end users.

* Researched and wrote copy for 80 percent of all TV manuals within strict time constraints.
* Created a modular technique which permitted consolidation of two or more similar manuals to one, resulting in major savings in translating, printing and handling costs.
* Worked directly with all levels of staff and management.

Dukane Corporation, St. Charles, IL   1986-1990
Technical Writer
Responsible for in-depth research and the writing of installation and operating manuals, service manuals & specification sheets for communication systems.
Prepared custom drawings and layouts with desktop publishing systems listed above.
Worked directly with design engineers in all departments.

* Conducted research of materials for all advanced product lines.
* Reduced technical writing staff by 20 percent through implementation of an on-line desktop publishing system.
* Speeded turnaround time for new product documentation by 25 percent.

Tree and Root Engineering, Naperville, IL　　　　　　　　　　　　　　　1979-1986
Project Control Coordinator
Organized an entire project control task force for job scheduling, cost control and material/document management.

* 　　Monitored and improved the progress of engineering, procurement and construction activities related to the construction of power plants and oil refineries.
* 　　Reorganized the document control system and developed a new methods/control manual; reduced labor costs 30 percent and labor hours from 18,000 to 10,000 per project.

Universal Petroleum Products, Des Plaines, IL　　　　　　　　　　　　　1977-1979
Engineering Services Supervisor
Developed specifications and handled bidder/vendor relations and expediting in a professional manner.
Recorded project documentation and prepared/analyzed cost reports.
Documented and analyzed variances against control budgets.

* 　　Established and implemented engineering administrative procedures.

Southrop Corporation, Rolling Meadows, IL　　　　　　　　　　　　　　1973-1979
Engineer
Primarily responsible for component evaluation and the preparation of specifications and cost estimates.
Assisted in equipment analysis and selection.
Prepared test reports and verified compliance of materials, design and workmanship to specifications.

* 　　Verified - and reported on - the ability of test items to perform satisfactorily in various/adverse environmental conditions.
* 　　Assisted in production of Electronic Countermeasure Sets used in F-15 aircraft.

AT&T, Rolling Meadows, IL　　　　　　　　　　　　　　　　　　　　　　1969-1973
Equipment Engineer
Prepared and issued specifications, engineering standards and installation procedures.
Processed/wrote software data for operating companies and provided computer services to telephone companies in four states.

* 　　Implemented hardware and software applications for communication systems.

EDUCATION:　　Keller Graduate School, Chicago, IL　　　　　　　　　　　　　　　1982-1985
　　　　　　　　　Attended courses towards MBA

　　　　　　　　　Elmhurst College, Elmhurst, IL　　　　　　　　　　　　　　　　　　　　1977
　　　　　　　　　B.S. Degree -- Business Administration

RALPH SHARK

COMBINATION

73 Nautilus Lane
Hanover Park, IL 60103
708/555-6393

OBJECTIVE:	A position utilizing skills developed in the railroad and shipping industries.
EXPERIENCE:	■ Comprehensive background in delivery administration, merchandise inspection, returns and dispatching.
	■ Skilled in customer service, order tracking and billing; interact with customers and resolve problems in a personalized and professional manner.
	■ Recruit, train and supervise employees; coordinate work loads and schedules.

EMPLOYMENT:

<u>The Home Delivery Service,</u> Des Plaines, IL   4/90-Present
Inspector   6/90-Present
Responsible for check in of delivery trucks and inspection of returned merchandise/trade-in items.
Utilize automated computer systems for manifest preparation and record keeping.
Field incoming calls from customers and resolve delivery issues.
Make calls to customers to verify deliveries and payment arrangements.
Coordinate driver schedules, cancellations and route changes.

Bay Checker   4/90-6/90
Duties included organizing/loading the dock area to meet delivery requirements.
Confirmed the accuracy of merchandise orders and maintained delivery records.
Inspected appliances, furniture and other merchandise items to verify condition.

<u>St. Paul & Pacific/Soo Line Railroad,</u> Bensenville, IL   6/71-11/89
Intermodal Clerk/Yard Clerk   1/79-11/89
Processed shipping orders and coordinated train departures.
Prepared bills off of bills of lading and maintained accurate records.
Handled filing of waybills and switch lists.

Reconsigning/Weigh Clerk   9/78-1/79
Duties included reconsigning cars for industries and their brokers.
Handled rate shipping charges on bi and tri-level cars.
Prepared bills of lading and weigh certificates; recorded carload weights and checked for overloads.

Yard Clerk/Industry Clerk   6/71-9/78
Provided customer assistance and maintained clerical records.
Handled billing and compiled information on empty car availability, route schedules, releases, car transfers and switches.

EDUCATION: <u>East Layden High School,</u> Franklin Park, IL   Graduate

STEVEN J. NAYOB   *COMBINATION*

110 Mural Lane
Mt. Prospect, IL 60056   708/555-0211

OBJECTIVE: **Loan Officer**
A position where proven analytical skills would be utilized.

EXPERIENCE:
- More than three years in cost analyses, credit and securities operations, including full responsibility for account tracking and updating.

- Experience in construction loan administration; familiar with all related credit approval forms and procedures.

- Compile and present spreadsheets and reports; skilled in Lotus, Harvard Graphics, WordPerfect, Paradox, PC tools and various database management systems.

- Assist in marketing, portfolio management and risk analysis; perform wire transfers and general administration with legal, credit and collateral personnel; provide full customer service and support.

- Skilled in general accounting, collections and written/oral customer correspondence.

EMPLOYMENT: <u>First Chicago Bank,</u> Chicago, IL   1988-Present

Marketing Assistant / Second Assistant Loan Officer   1990-Present
Work directly with loan officers and provide support in credit and administration for major construction loans.
Manage a 20-PC network and design/utilize cash flow models on R.E.P.A., a computerized real estate project analysis system.
Train personnel in computer system use on a continual basis.

* Communicate with staff and assist in cash management, as well as the administration of letters of credit.
* Interface with lenders and loan personnel in a personalized, yet professional manner.

Work station   1988-1990
Responsible for order expediting and the constant review/management of risks and cash flows.
Tracked outstanding accounts and the timeliness of funding for specific projects.
Performed data input, wire transfers and various credit-related functions.

* Completed bank training in internal credit procedures.

<u>Loftus and Omera,</u> Chicago, IL 1987-1988
Accounting Assistant
Transferred and verified accounting records on a computerized system for a major chemical testing firm.

<u>Superior Temporary,</u> Elk Grove Village, IL Summers, 1986-1987
Warehouseman
Processed orders and worked with management in a prompt, professional manner.

<u>Jeffrey Laundromat,</u> Carbondale, IL 2/86-5/86
Manager
Accepted all profit/loss responsibilities for sales, accounting and procedures at this coin-operated laundromat.

EDUCATION: <u>Southern Illinois University,</u> Carbondale, IL 1991
B.S. Degree -- Finance and Business

* Completed a major project involving an in-depth case study simulating a business. Planned and implemented effective financial controls and improved levels of productivity.
* Raised status of the company to 18th from 57th.

Activities:

* Floor Representative, 1983
* Student Life Advisor - Student Orientation, 1983
* Vice President, Hall Council, 1984
* Social Chairman, Intervarsity Christian Fellowship, 1985
* President, Intervarsity Christian Fellowship, 1986 and 1987.
* Speaker Committee Member, Financial Management Association, 1988.

5139 Mohawk Street	**JAMES NECKI**	*COMBINATION*
Lake Zurich, IL 60047		708/555-8231

LAW ENFORCEMENT / AVIATION

EXPERIENCE:
- Direct experience in criminal investigations, including searches and subject interviewing; well-versed in customs regulations and procedures.

- Accredited Military Customs Agent; handle confiscations/seizures and apprehensions of violent and non-violent subjects.

- Private Pilot's License: 180 Hours with Instrument Rating; experience with Cessna and Beechcraft.

MILITARY:

U.S. Army, Nurnberg, Germany　　　　　　　　　　　　　　　　11/84-11/87
Military Policeman / Investigator　　　　　　　　　　　　　　7/86-11/87
Conducted numerous investigations of black market trading between soldiers and German civilians.
Handled surveillance and tracking of subjects.
* Apprehended, arrested and interviewed perpetrators and seized all types of goods: tobacco, alcohol, clothing, electronics and various weapons.
* As Accredited U.S. Military Customs Agent, conducted searches and cleared aircraft in Europe bound for the U.S.

CIVILIAN EMPLOYMENT:

Buehler YMCA, Palatine, IL　　　　　　　　　　　　　　　Pt. Time 12/91-Present
Building Supervisor
Manage building facilities, security and personnel.

Colonial Hospital Supply Co., Lake Zurich, IL　　　　　　　Pt. Time 7/88-7/91
Receiving / Warehouseman
Handled prompt receiving and storage of hospital supplies.
Updated and maintained inventory reports on a daily basis.

Safari Club, Schaumburg, IL　　　　　　　　　　　　　　Pt. Time 8/88-8/89
Doorman
Maintained safe and secure operations at this large capacity night club; managed drunk/disorderly patrons in a professional manner.

Guardsmark Security Services, Libertyville, IL　　　　　　　　　　　1/88-8/88
Security Guard

EDUCATION:

Lewis University, Romeoville, IL
B.S. Degree -- Aviation Administration　　　　　　　　　　　Graduate: 5/92
Overall GPA: 3.3/4.0　Major GPA: 3.5/4.0
* Completed extensive flying in aircraft listed above through the Aviation Administration.

MILES DAVIS   *COMBINATION*

4413 Willow Avenue
Deerfield, IL 60015   708/555-9246

OBJECTIVE: **Restaurant Management**
A position where profit-building skills would be utilized.

EXPERIENCE:
- Proven abilities in the setup and management of restaurant and hotel operations, including full P&L responsibilities.

- Manage all aspects of budgets, forecasting, purchasing and marketing; track sales of individual food and beverage items on a daily basis.

- Handle payroll, AP/AR, general ledger maintenance and inventory control; implement labor and cost controls; create daily sales and P&L reports on computerized systems.

- Conduct on-the-job training and supervision of front and back-house staff in food preparation, sanitation and effective customer service.

- Plan and implement menus for banquets and special events; coordinate co-op and in-house advertising and sales promotions.

EMPLOYMENT: Coor's Pub, Chicago, IL   1990-Present
Manager
Train and supervise more than 80 employees in all front & back house operations for this major downtown restaurant.
Conduct group and individual training of kitchen and wait staff; formulate job classifications; develop work incentives and evaluate worker performance.

  * Create daily P&L statements and manage all general accounting functions: AP/AR, payroll and general ledgers.
  * Oversee employee benefit and insurance activities.
  * Utilize a TEK computer to track daily sales of individual food and beverage items.
  * Perform cost-effective purchasing of all food, beverage, equipment and supplies, with excellent vendor relations.

Davis' Grand Hotel, Wauconda, IL   1988-1990
Owner / General Manager
Responsible for all sales, marketing and more than 30 employees at this full service restaurant.
Supervised all customer service activities.

  * Designed and marketed banquet plans for a variety of businesses and community groups

Davis' Pine Log Restaurant, Skokie, IL   1972-1988
General Manager / Owner
Directed hiring, training and scheduling functions for more than 70 employees, including introduction of a three-step on-the-job training program with seminars and video instruction.
Conducted monthly waitstaff meetings for employee feedback and brainstorming to improve operations and morale.
Formalized job classifications and evaluated worker performance.
Worked directly with bookkeeping staff to track and process all data related to payroll, AP/AR, cost controls, food and liquor.

* Responsible for all marketing, promotions and advertising.
* Designed employee recognition programs and increased the sale of wine, dessert and after-drink purchases.
* Increased sales through co-op advertising programs with American Express Corp, local beer/wine purveyors and food vendors.
* Improved banquet sales and promotions with package plans for numerous organizations, including civic groups and large businesses: Marshall Fields & Company, Gingiss Formal Wear, Seno & Sons, schools, churches and synagogues.

At this restaurant *and* at the Grand Hotel:

* Reduced payroll preparation costs 5 percent by using outside data processing services.
* Lowered payroll 3 percent by restructuring salaried worker's status to an hourly rate scale.
* Decreased liquor costs 4 percent by restructuring purchasing procedures.
* Lowered discount rates charged by major credit card companies by 50 percent.
* Reduced liability insurance premiums by 10 percent.
* Consolidated total insurance premiums with one common carrier.

CERTIFICATION: State of Illinois Sanitation Certified.

EDUCATION: Loyola University of Chicago, Chicago, IL
B.A. Degree -- Business Administration   1972

Loras College, Dubuque, IA   1971
Completed Business Administration Studies

ROGER ARCHAMBALDT, CIC, ARM

CHRONOLOGICAL With Conservative Summary

151 Falls Street
Elgin, IL 60123

708/555-8765

RISK MANAGEMENT AND UNDERWRITING PROFESSIONAL

Executive-level skills in risk management, innovative problem solving and operations management.
Thirteen years of diversified insurance experience includes management, underwriting, and claims handling.

EXPERIENCE

Chico National Insurance Company (A subsidiary of Peterbilt International Transportation Corp.)
Rolling Meadows, IL   1989-Present

Vice President, Underwriting and Administration
Determine and manage underwriting guidelines, loss control, policy rating and processing for all lines of business in 48 states. Directly responsible for supervising 52 employees and administering a $2.8 million department budget.

- Developed and implemented underwriting manuals and procedures for Long Haul Trucking, Auto Lease & Rental, and General Agent Guidelines.
- Reduced loss ratio by 3.1 percent during Fiscal Year 1990 and 4.9 percent during FY 1991.
- Diverse coverages include property, garage and auto liability, worker's compensation and umbrella.
- $100,000 under budget in 1991, during a significant $3.9 million increase in written premiums.
- Initiated and structured an in-house Loss Control Department.
- Highly skilled at motivating and focusing activities of diverse departments to accomplish goals.
- Active Member of the N.A.I.I. Trucker's Committee since 1989.

National Farmers Union Insurance Companies - Denver, CO	1983-1989
Commercial Underwriting Manager	1989
Senior Account Manager - Corporate Accounts	1985-1989
Account Manager (Underwriter)	1983-1985

Directly responsible for all aspects of risk selection and underwriting for Farm Cooperatives and Telephone Companies with premiums ranging from $50,000 to $1 million.

- Co-authored the company package policy for Special Accounts.
- Diverse coverages included: directors' and officers', property, general and auto liability, workers' compensation and umbrella.
- Developed and implemented a procedure manual for General Agents and Commercial Underwriters.

Progressive Casualty Insurance Company - Denver, CO   1979-1983

Senior Claims Adjuster
Controlled each claim from inception to settlement for both high risk auto, motorcycle and property lines.

- Assessed and established loss reserves.
- Negotiated settlements with claimants and/or representing attorneys.
- Successfully covered a multistate territory.

Proctor and Gamble Distribution Company - Englewood, CO   1978-1979

Institutional Sales Representative
Responsible for the sale of Commercial/Institutional Cleaning and Soap products for Colorado and Wyoming.

- Facilitated the introduction of "Comet Liquid".

Green River High School - Green River, WY   1976-1978

Teacher/Coordinator of Distributive Education (Marketing)
Responsible for teaching three marketing courses and coordinating 45 students in off-site, part-time employment.

- Promoted to Department Head of Program in 1977.
- Sponsor of DECA Club (extracurricular).
- Member of the School District Curriculum Committee.

EDUCATION

University of Wyoming, Laramie, WY
Completed several courses towards a Masters Degree in Business Administration.

Colorado State University (CSU), Ft. Collins, CO
B.E. Degree, Education   Graduated 1976
- Graduated First in Class with Highest Distinction.

CERTIFICATIONS / AWARDS

Associate in Risk Management (ARM)   1988
- Award for Academic Excellence at CPCU Awards Ceremony.

Certified Insurance Counselor (CIC)   1985

American Educational Institute   1983
Certified for completion of Legal Principals Course.

QUIGLEY SELLICK *COMBINATION*

3379 S. Rock Lane
Bloomingdale, IL 60108   708/555-0275

REAL ESTATE APPRAISER

EXPERIENCE:
- Completed studies in Real Estate Appraisal Principles at The Appraisal Institute in Chicago; working towards SRA designation.

- Strong interpersonal, communication and customer service skills; able to effectively interact with individuals for program planning and implementation.

EDUCATION: **Bachelor of Science Degree:** Political Science
Minor in Criminal Justice Sciences
Illinois State University, Normal, IL 1990

- Delta Chi Fraternity: GAMMA Committee Representative, PR Committee
  Fall 1988 to Fall 1990
- Illinois State University Law Club
  Fall 1988 to Spring 1989
- Illinois State University Tae Kwon Do Club
  Fall 1985 to Spring 1987

With the Risk Management Committee under GAMMA:
- Implemented and organized Greek Designated Driver Program in conjunction with local drinking establishments.
- Developed and designed pamphlets to provide necessary information to promote responsibility in planning social gatherings.

EMPLOYMENT: C.P.S. Incorporated, Westchester, IL
Research Assistant   1991-Present
Maintain thousands of files and a computer-based employee tracking system for the M.I.S./Mainframe Division, as well as full administrative support.

Houlihan's Restaurant, Bloomingdale, IL
Waiter   1990-1991
Coordinated side-station duties, assisted in problem solving, served as host.

P.A. Bergner, Bloomington, IL
Sales Associate   1989-1989
Employed aggressive sales techniques to consistently achieve/exceed weekly goals; closed department; provided customer service.

ARCO AM/PM Mini Market, Hinsdale, IL
Assistant Manager   1985-1986
Trained, scheduled, and supervised up to 10 employees. Responsible for inventory control, purchasing, and cash management.

DENNIS M. WILLIE   COMBINATION

222 Fairview Lane   708/555-2431
Bartlett, IL 60103

OBJECTIVE: **Plant Manager**
A position utilizing skills in a wide range of production environments.

EXPERIENCE:
- Proven technical and management skills in job-shop functions including Class A progressive die, CNC and fabrication work for all types of projects.

- Hire, train and supervise workers in customer service and part/product finishing, manufacturing and quality control with lathes, grinders, mills, EDMs and CNC equipment.

- Determine and meet customer's specific needs with solid communication skills; read and interpret blueprints and work with technical staff at all levels.

- Manage functions related to inventory and cost control on Hewlett Packard PC systems; track projects, due dates and virtually all plant operations.

EMPLOYMENT: GPS Industries, Inc., Melrose Park, IL   1987-Present
Plant Manager
Responsible for all plant operations and more than 38 employees at this job shop -- specializing in part and tool fabrication for the aerospace and automotive industries.
Create and analyze computer printouts for due dates, labor tracking and effective customer service.
Handle worker performance reviews and motivation.
Coordinate all production operations; schedule personnel and the maintenance of:

--	AGIE Wire Machines	--	CNC equipment
--	Sinker EDMs	--	Cylindrical & Surface Grinders
--	Turning Centers	--	Lathes
--	Machining Centers	--	Mills

* Maintain excellent product/part quality standards and tolerances.
* In charge of both day and night shifts, 1987-1990.

AGIE, U.S.A., Addison, IL   1983-1987
Application Engineer
Conducted group and individual end-user training in the use of specialized wire (AGIE) machines for steel cutting.
Utilized a strong knowledge of tool & die procedures.

* Researched and wrote a training manual for the use of 3-D Lama software.
* Conducted group and individual training of all customers in computer system operation.

Dennis M. Willie

Tri-Link Metals, Elmhurst, IL	1982-1983 and 1972-1977
Lead Die Maker	1982-1983

Created Class A, progressive dies for a wide range of applications.
Supervised 1-2 apprentices.

Restaurant Business, Carol Stream and Lombard, IL   1978-1982
Owner / President
In charge of all bookkeeping, purchasing, personnel and sales.

Lonnagen Die Corp., Broadview, IL   1977-1978
Foreman
Responsible for up to 22 employees and all tool and die production activity.
Purchased all materials and supplies for the toolroom.

*   Hired, trained and scheduled staff and organized production for peak efficiency.

Prior Experience as Die Maker and Application Engineer at:

American Tool & Manufacturing

Tech Tool & Die

EDUCATION:

Tool & Die Institute, Park Ridge, IL   Five Years
Earned Certificate for completion of numerous courses.

Whitewater State University, WI   One Year
Completed courses in English, Math and Psychology.

Badger High School, Lake Geneva, IL
Graduate

JOHN MELLON   COMBINATION

331 Phillippi Drive
Elgin, IL 60120   708/555-1199

OBJECTIVE: **Management: International Freight Forwarding**
A position where profit-building skills would be utilized.

EXPERIENCE:
- Proven management skills in virtually all import/export operations, including full profit/loss responsibilities.

- Hire, train and supervise staff and management in customs regulations, freight forwarding, routing, sales and marketing.

- Budget planning and sales forecasting; skilled in financial statement preparation and analysis; familiar with Lotus.

- Experience in full warehouse and multi-site supervision.

EMPLOYMENT: Tony Corporation, Des Plaines, IL   3/89-3/92

Regional Vice President
Responsible for six midwest offices and more than 60 employees in the Chicago office; directed six managers and their staff, a total of 117 employees.
Created and administered all budgets for the Chicago office and analyzed/approved budgets for all six offices.
Directed domestic/international air freight, customs brokerage, ocean import/export, container services and inbound/outbound ocean freight.
In charge of overall sales and productivity, including staff training and motivation.

* Managed all operations at a 32,000 s.f. warehouse.
* Gross 1991 profit exceeded $4 million in the Chicago office alone.
* Reduced staff while increasing productivity and speed of order processing.
* Planned, implemented and improved all sales and marketing strategies with an extensive knowledge of competitors, air/sea carriers and the clientele.

Rainey Robinson Company, Bensenville, IL   1970-3/89

Vice President / Regional Manager   1984-3/89
Directed sales, marketing and all shipping & import/export operations for this firm specializing in customs brokerage, ocean shipping and sales.
Managed over 60 staff and managers at locations in Cleveland, Detroit, Chicago and St. Louis.

Midwest Regional Manager 1975-1984
Accepted full responsibility for all duties listed above.

*   Personally setup and opened the highly successful St. Louis and Detroit offices.

Branch Manager 1970-1975
In charge of the Chicago branch office with more than 35 support personnel and supervisors.

Nettles & Company, Bensenville, IL 1967-1970

Manager / Corporate Secretary
Responsible for all export operations and air/ocean freight.
Directly involved in the setup of this entire company, including office procedure planning, market penetration and sales.

*   Assisted in budget preparation, sales forecasting and financial planning.

EDUCATION: Northwestern Illinois University, Evanston, IL
Successful completion of two seminars in Transportation, including training in railroad and import/export operations.

Xerox Corporation
Completed training in professional selling skills.

Dale Carnegie Management Course
Completed extensive Management training programs.

High School Graduate

PERSONAL: Enjoy Golf, Boating, Music and all Sports.

NORMAN MAILER   *COMBINATION*

325 Arbor Lane   708/555-2563
Bloomingdale, IL 60108

PURCHASING MANAGEMENT

EXPERIENCE:
- More than 13 years in virtually all aspects of purchasing, including full responsibility for department setup, procedures and management.

- Experience in new product development, cost reduction and inventory control; proficient in MRP II and JIT system implementation and user training.

- Skilled in vendor/material sourcing and price negotiation; organize buyers and suppliers in major international markets.

- Plan and conduct vendor quality audits; organize component purchasing and subcontracting procedures.

- Hire, train and supervise buyers and support staff at all levels of experience.

EMPLOYMENT: Superdudes, Inc., Roselle, IL   1985-Present
Purchasing Manager
Manage all aspects of a multimillion dollar purchasing department for a major manufacturer of equipment for the fast food industry.
Direct buyers and support staff in the sourcing and purchase of raw materials, electronic components, plastics, machine parts and sheet metal goods.
Work directly with engineers and department managers; supervise purchasing functions related to new product development, contract negotiations and subcontracting for machining operations.
Aggressively research and secure competitive prices on all required parts and components, resulting in substantial cost savings.

* Successfully installed computerized MRP II systems within the purchasing department.
* Researched and implemented software systems to evaluate purchased product cost, availability, on-time delivery and quality on a department and company-wide basis.
* Sourced new products and greatly reduced preliminary costs.
* Perform quality audits of suppliers; provide corrective action and follow-up audits.
* Effectively cross-trained personnel to ensure adequate coverage of all commodities.
* Created, implemented and improved bills of material.
* Initiated a cost reduction program with several suppliers; lowered costs while improving both quality and speed of delivery.

<u>Cylinder Component, Inc.</u>, Franklin Park, IL 1981-1985
Purchasing Agent
Established an entire purchasing department from the ground floor for this multimillion dollar producer of air and hydraulic cylinder accessories.
Planned and implemented policies and procedures.
* Purchased castings and forgings; maintained excellent part quality.
* Aggressively sourced component parts & supplies.
* Reported directly to company president.

<u>Miller Fluid Power Corporation, Inc.</u>, Bensenville, IL 1966-1981
Various Purchasing positions, most recent first:

Purchasing Department Supervisor
Managed a purchasing department of 14 for this firm which manufactured and distributed air and hydraulic cylinders and related equipment.
* Reduced inventory by 10 percent; ensured a continuous availability of parts.
* Updated machining practices and reduced rejected, subcontracted parts by 25 percent; lowered related costs by 10 percent.
* Converted production of various parts from casting to forging; reduced rejection rate and machining costs by 10 percent; lowered lead time by 50 percent.

Senior Buyer
Trained and evaluated new buyers and assisted in a steady transition to a more complex product line.
* Worked directly with engineers in part design and tolerance updating; saved 30 percent annually and reduced costs in custom part production while speeding delivery time.
* Assisted engineers in material upgrades, resulting in annual savings of 25 percent on piece parts and 10 percent on rejects damaged in assembly.
* Developed a new product line introduced six months prior to the competition; substantially increasing gross sales.

Buyer
Recommended alternatives and upgrades for steel and plastic materials, monitored costs, sourced vendors and created competitive pricing.

Order Writer

EDUCATION: <u>College of DuPage</u>, Glen Ellyn, IL
A.A.S. Degree 1979

<u>Oliver Wright MPP II Classes</u> Six Months

JENNY L. CAPER *COMBINATION*

114 Old Country Way
Wauconda, IL 60084

708/555-9521

OBJECTIVE: **Radiology:**
A position where proven supervisory skills would be utilized.

EXPERIENCE:
- More than six years in MRI department functions, including full responsibility for patient relations and staff hiring, training & supervision.

- Schedule and organize all MRI procedures; skilled in the use of G.E. 1.5 and .5 Tesla Technicare scanners for brain, cervical, thoracic, abdomen, lumbar spine and extremity analysis.

- Planned and conducted an MRI certification program at Triton College, 8/89; Co-Author of an article which appeared in *Radiology* magazine.

EMPLOYMENT: Redtown Radiology Institute, Highland Park, IL   7/85-Present
Chief Technologist - Magnetic Resonance Imaging Department
Responsible for all MRI department activities and the training, supervision and coordination of up to 10 technologists and darkroom staff.
Schedule and expedite all patients and work directly with physicians; review patient's clinical history for scanning and photography.
Operate remote and operator consoles, as well as boot terminal equipment; select and modify technical factors as required.

Supervise all documentation and filing procedures, as well as examinations listed above for inpatients and outpatients.
Prepare room equipment, medications and infusion materials.
Question patients and thoroughly explain all procedures.
* Increase MRI patient throughput by 10 percent each year since 1985.
* Reduced MRI staff turnover by 40 percent.

EDUCATION: Lake Forest College, Lake Forest, IL   1981-1983
Successful completion of courses in Biochemistry.

SEMINARS & TRAINING: The Medical College of Wisconsin   4/90
Courses included FastScan MRI and clinical applications of gradient echos.
Attended a pathology demonstration of spin echo/gradient echo crossovers.

McAllister Business Courses   6/91
Completed an eight-week course in Effective Time Management.

PUBLICATION: *Radiology* - 169 (p) 83
Co-Author of "H-1 MR Spectroscopy of Human Tumors In Vivo.

225 S. Greenwood Avenue	**SAMUEL PORT**	*COMBINATION*
Palatine, IL 60067		708/555-7895

OBJECTIVE: Field Service / Technical Support

EXPERIENCE:
- Handle component and system-level repair and testing of electronic equipment; work directly with engineers and production staff at all levels.

- Assist in procedure planning and implementation, as well as job scheduling and business system streamlining.

- Plan and conduct sales presentations with professional communication skills; negotiate contracts and determine/meet client's specific product needs.

- Direct experience in advertising, promotions and general marketing; proven ability to develop referral business through personalized customer service.

EMPLOYMENT:

Marietta Corporation, Rolling Meadows, IL   8/79-1/91
Senior Electronic Technician   1984-1/91
Involved in the development and sale of radar and advanced avionics equipment to the U.S. government.
Documented all product specifications and functions through technical writing of reports; analyzed and corrected design flaws in a variety of systems for advanced bomber and fighter aircraft.
* Conducted in-depth contract and blueprint interpretation for the clientele.
* Responsible for efficient production scheduling through interface with senior-level management and engineers.
* Trained numerous workers in the use of testing and production equipment.
* Analyzed and streamlined all related production and sales procedures.

Electronic Technician   1982-1984
Maintained excellent product quality through testing with class "B" equipment, including oscilloscopes, and spectrum & spectral analyzers.

Repair Technician   1980-1982
Solderer / Assembler   1979-1980

Mr. G's, Palatine, IL   4/90-Present
Owner/Operator
Responsible for all sales and marketing at this painting and remodeling service.
Quote prices and negotiate sales contracts; design/place creative advertising and promotions.
Train and supervise personnel in effective customer service and work procedures.

EDUCATION: William Rainey Harper College, Palatine, IL   1985
Completed more than 40 credit hours in Electronics and Mathematics

High School Graduate

DEAN JAIN   *COMBINATION*

4333 Washington Street
Bartlett, IL 60103   708/555-0795

OBJECTIVE: Architect
A position utilizing training and experience in drafting and project management.

SUMMARY:
- Extensive training in the design of residential/commercial buildings and steel structures, as well as plot surveying and layout.

- More than three years in design, drafting and blueprint development, including full project management responsibilities.

- Experience in job costing, price quoting and professional customer service; plan and conduct written & oral presentations with excellent communication skills.

EMPLOYMENT: Snap Connectors, Elk Grove Village, IL   1988-Present
Engineering Draftsman - Engineering Services
Responsible for designing and drafting a wide range of electrical connectors for automotive, industrial and ordnance applications.
Effectively manage projects from concept to completion, including extensive customer relations for design updates and troubleshooting.
Perform full project cost estimating and price quoting.
Compile and present written proposals, estimates and presentations for the clientele.

* Developed configurations for office floors and efficient placement of computer workstations, tables and filing systems.
* As blueprint department back-up, distributed blueprints and plans to various companies and plants nationwide.

Crawford Risk Management, Schaumburg, IL   1987-1988
Documentation Department
Worked extensively with adjusters and organized, updated & prepared courtroom files on a computer system.

Sears Credit Central, Schaumburg, IL   1977-1987
Customer Service Representative
Responsible for heavy telephone communications with customers regarding credit and account status.
Updated and maintained numerous files on a computer system.

EDUCATION: University of Illinois, Chicago, IL   Graduated 8/91
B.S. Degree: Architecture   GPA: 3.5/4.0

William Rainey Harper College, Palatine, IL
Successful completion of Architectural courses, evenings, 1986-1988.
* Taught classes in Architecture, including student motivation and evaluation.

	NIKKI ZELLO	*COMBINATION*
228 N. Walnut Lane Schaumburg, IL 60194		708/555-7063

OBJECTIVE: **Flight Attendant: American Airlines**
Willing to travel or relocate.

EXPERIENCE:
- More than two years in customer service and professional communications, including responsibility for troubleshooting and work flow organizing.
- Strong knowledge of first-aid; Certificate: Red Cross Junior Lifesaving.
- Speak conversational German; traveled throughout Germany, Austria, Canada, Hawaii and the continental U.S.
- Height: 5'7", 125 lbs; professional modeling experience for a major fragrance company; selected for advanced modeling courses at the Barbizon School of Modeling.

EMPLOYMENT: Apple Garden Restaurant, Bloomingdale, IL   1/91-Present
Hostess
Organize and track seating for hundreds of customers daily at this busy Italian restaurant.
Greet customers in a professional manner and provide prompt, courteous service.
*   Train new employees in all hosting and seating procedures.

Carlos Murphy's, Schaumburg, IL   1/90-12/90
Hostess
Developed customer volume reports every 30 minutes.
Greeted and directed hundreds of patrons to their tables quickly and politely.
*   Answer telephone calls quickly and professionally.

Schaumburg Park District, Schaumburg, IL   Winter, 1987-1988
Ice Skating Supervisor
Monitored skaters and the safety of skating conditions.
Completed accidents and performed on-the-spot first aid as needed.

EDUCATION: William Rainey Harper College, Palatine, IL
Completed a Psychology course; enrolled in Typing and Reading courses.

Barbizon School of Modeling, Chicago, IL
Graduated from Modeling courses, 1989

Schaumburg High School Graduate

PERSONAL: **Skated Competitively** for ten years, including six years in precision skating.
Church Usher at Church of the Holy Spirit, Schaumburg.
Enjoy skating, skiing and bicycling.

JOHN D. WALTERS   CHRONOLOGICAL/*Brief Summary*

922 Wakeby Lane
Schaumburg, IL 60193   708/555-5474

OBJECTIVE:	**Chief of Police**
	A position utilizing proven leadership skills in law enforcement.
SUMMARY:	▪ More than 12 years in law enforcement, including responsibility for special program planning/implementation and officer coordination.
EXPERIENCE:	Cook County Sheriffs Department, Chicago, IL 11/91-Present

Deputy Sheriff

Responsible for spearheading a special O.U.I Task Force, including the screening and management of 13 officers in the detection and apprehension of impaired operators. Area of scope includes the Chain O' Lakes water ways.
Task Force management duties are in addition to regular patrol unit responsibilities.

Village of Gilberts, IL   7/90-11/91

Police Officer -- currently on leave of absence

In addition to regular Police Officer duties, effectively instituted and managed *Project Management for Accreditation*, which included the writing and implementation of policies and procedures.
Responsible for building interdepartmental skills and relations within the Gilberts Police Department and with the Sheriff's department.
Coordinated seven employees and their accreditation, involving extensive training and development.
Assisted in developing computer software for the networking of records, as well as the purchase of related hardware.

* Demonstrated the need for -- and initiated -- a Mobile Data Terminal (MDT) system and trained personnel in its use.
* Developed and managed the A.I.M. (Alliance Against Intoxicated Motorists) and M.A.D.D. (Mothers Against Drunk Driving) programs.
* Initiated the *Notice of Minor Violation* program, which increased the General Revenue Fund by 80 percent.
* Started a Z.A.P. Program to encourage youth to reject commercials that encourage drinking.
* Supervised fundraising efforts for the 1991 Gilbert's Police Department Benevolent Association. Committed to contacting local businesses to raise money for equipment. Increased revenue from the previous year from several hundred dollars to more than $3,000.
* Wrote a grant for the department this year to the Illinois Department of transportation for the purchase of a breathalyzer.
* As Field Training officer, trained new officers in department policies and procedures and taught interdepartment classes.

*   Planned and implemented procedures for a Warrant's Program, and physically served warrants as needed.

United States Department of Energy, Various Locations   1/89-7/90
Federal Officer
Responsible for the protection of life and property of federal employees at nuclear installations. Currently on leave of absence.

Venture Transportation, Inc., Schaumburg, IL   3/84-8/90
President / CEO
In charge of all operations and facilities for this transportation, brokerage and forwarding service, including fiscal/executive management, sales and marketing. Recruited carriers, acquired real estate and developed/administered budgets.

* Implemented a computer system for dispatch and commodities control, as well as programs for warehousing, physical distribution, storage and consolidation.
* Worked closely with personnel in air freight, LTL/full truck shipments and rail.
* Managed sales and marketing, including brochures, radio and telecommunications; wrote sales materials and contracts for carriers.

Police Officer and Deputy Sheriff, Various Departments   1977-1987
Gained more than ten years of experience in all aspects of patrol and law enforcement, including patrol duty on rotating shifts and traffic enforcement.
Enforced DUI programs and assisted in detective work.
* Worked in the jail, served warrants and acted as road deputy.

SPECIALIZED TRAINING:
* Project Management for Accreditation
* Illinois State Police Training Academy
* Missouri Highway Patrol Training Academy
* Federal Officer's Training Academy
* Northern Illinois Truck Enforcement School
* Breathalyzer Operator - Certified IDPH
* Legal aspects of department discipline
* Financial investigation/white collar crime
* Team building
* Criminal procedure and civil liability
* Domestic violence/crisis intervention
* Labor relations: management and labor issues

EDUCATION: William Rainey Harper College
LaSalle University, Juris Doctor Student
Attended several law enforcement management seminars in April of 1991, which included small to medium-sized department management classes held at Northwestern University in Evanston, IL.

FRED REYERSON *COMBINATION*

432 Bridle Terrace
Addison, IL 60101   708/555-2951

OBJECTIVE: **Claims Adjuster**
A position utilizing proven abilities in data management and communication.

EXPERIENCE:
- Skilled in database management and operations analysis in high-pressure situations; perform audits of customer accounts, legal files and airline flight information.

- Thorough working knowledge of CICS/Unimatic, TSO/Focus computer systems and Lotus 1-2-3.

- Research and write status reports on a full range of operations for corporate management; train assistants on contractual research procedures.

EMPLOYMENT: United Airlines Inc., Elk Grove Village, IL   1989-Present
Source Data Controller   5/91-Present
Accurately process flight data including passenger, cargo and flight schedules.
Assist group manager in streamlining weekly operations; promptly correct improperly formatted data.

   *   Earned Certificate for no sick days or late attendance.
   *   Promoted to this position from:

Administrative Assistant   12/89-5/91
Maintained contract and document files in the corporate legal library.
Identified incomplete contracts and initiated corrective action.

Household Bank, Schaumburg, IL   9/89-12/89
Customer Service Representative
Responsible for general financial transactions and customer relations.
Handled customer account maintenance and data entry/retrieval; familiar with IBM 4704 Teller System.

Vapor Corporation, Niles, IL   1985-1987
Assembler
Assembled and/or repaired bus and train doors.
Carried a full college course load while working 20 hours each week.

EDUCATION: University of Illinois at Chicago, Chicago, IL   1985-1989
B.S. Degree - Mathematics

   *   Major GPA: 4.0/5.0
   *   Member of the Filipino Club
   *   Volunteer for the United Way Charitable Program, 1991

DAVID MILKE *COMBINATION*

3339 Hazelnut Drive
Streamwood, IL 60107

312/555-6591 Ofc.
708/555-1839 Res.

EXPERIENCE:

- More than 13 years of combined experience in domestic and international petrochemical and power plant construction, engineering, inspection and power plant outage work, including full department management and supervision.

- Work well in stressful and hostile environments at power and petrochemical plants in the Middle East.

- Proven abilities in virtually all phases of civil, mechanical, structural and electrical construction inspection.

- Develop and implement quality control procedures; conduct independent design verification reviews and ASME XI ISI baseline inspections of nuclear steam supply system (NSSS) piping.

- Experience as Lead Engineer; handle staff training, supervision and communications in a professional manner; work effectively with vendors and clientele at all levels of experience.

- Assist in writing and reviewing equipment specifications, welding/NDE procedures, and installation instructions; perform source surveillance inspections on nuclear and fossil plant equipment.

EMPLOYMENT:

Sergeant & Lefty Engineers, Chicago, IL 11/89-Present
Quality Control Engineer   Various Locations/Assignments:

Currently based in Chicago, IL - Q.C. Division 3/91-Present
Responsible for coordinating the submittal, review and acceptance of equipment vendor procedures for Point Aconi (fossil fuel) Power Station, Nova Scotia, Canada.

Tennessee Valley Authority, Watts Bar Nuclear Station
Spring City, TN 6/90-3/91
Performed electrical system and HVAC support walkdowns, including data compilation and the preparation of as-built field sketches.
Completed documentation for critical case evaluations in response to concerns generated by the NRC.

Chicago, IL 11/89-6/90
Coordinated the preparation of ASME code and material reconciliations for use at all Commonwealth Edison Nuclear Stations.
Provided full construction surveillance support at Schahfer Unit 14 during hot to cold precipitation modification.

Properties of America, Williamstown, MA 3/87-5/89
Associate Land Consultant, Senior Land Consultant, and Sales Manager.
Promoted to several positions in Maine, New Hampshire, and Vermont.
Planned and conducted sales presentations and supervised sales staff.
Assisted in marketing and the administration of budgets.

Stone & Webster Engineering Corporation, Various Locations/Assignments 3/74-4/86
Senior QC Engineer
Turkey Point Nuclear Power Plant, Homestead, FL 11/85-4/86
Performed radiography and film interpretation of piping systems, vessels and Welders' Test Coupons.

Superintendent of Quality Control 12/82-2/85
Aramco Marjan Gas Oil Separation Plant, Tanajib, Saudi Arabia
In charge of inspection aspects of this project from initial construction to final client acceptance.
Effectively controlled departmental budgets.
Supervised NDT contractors and vendor surveillance personnel.
Prepared certification of concrete batch plants and vendor qualifications.

QC Engineer 1/82-11/82
Field QC Headquarters Group, Boston, MA
Responsible for troubleshooting welding and code problems generated from field nuclear plant sites.
Wrote and revised new and existing FQC procedures and guidelines.

Welding Supervisor 9/80-12/81
Azzawiya Ethylene Complex, Ras Lanuf, Libya
Effectively monitored welding and NDT operations of contractors.
Coordinated the resolution of all technical problems through interface with London office and resolved routine site problems in absence of Senior Welding Engineer.

Associate QC Engineer 3/74-5/80
Shoreham Nuclear Power Plant, Wading River, NY
Primarily responsible for welding and NDT inspection on piping systems, supports and appurtances.

EDUCATION: Northeastern University, Boston, MA
Bachelor of Science Degree -- Industrial Technology, 1974

Wentworth Institute, Boston, MA
Associate of Applied Science Degree -- Aeronautical Technology, 1973

NDT Schools: Additional Training through Stone & Webster Engineering. Earned Level II NDT Certifications in: Ultrasonic, Radiography and Film Interpretation.

CARTER B. HODDING   *COMBINATION*

123 Hillside Court   708/555-4142 Res.
Bartlett, IL 60103   708/555-6548 Pager

OBJECTIVE: Paralegal
A position where communication and organizational skills would be utilized.

EXPERIENCE:
- Proven abilities in research, legal writing and the preparation of case studies using Westlaw and the Lexus system.

- Trained in real estate (Licensed Agent), probate and corporate/securities law, as well as contracts, litigation and adjudication.

- Experience in filings with various government agencies; provide trial and hearing support in a professional manner.

- Background in managing real estate, business, data and logistical matters.

EMPLOYMENT: Dryer, Brown & Platt, Washington, D.C.   1982-Present
Paralegal / Messenger
Provide trial/hearing support for this law office with up to 30 attorneys.
Conduct legal research at the Library Of Congress, as well as detailed investigations and legal writing.
Handle filings with the S.E.C. and the Departments Of Trade and Commerce.
* Act as messenger for important, time sensitive materials.
* Ensure accuracy of all written and oral communications.

Potomac Eagles Law Firm, Inc., Washington, D.C.   1974-1982
Paralegal
Specialized in corporate and tax law, litigation and real estate matters.
Incorporated new businesses, prepared corporate minutes and summarized depositions.
Analyzed and prepared real estate closing documents and checked facts and statements for appeals.
* Corresponded extensively with clients regarding case status and bankruptcy petitions.
* Drafted wills and performed detailed legal research.

Rotary Club International, Evanston, IL   1972-1974
General Office Clerk
Responsible for extensive correspondence writing and distribution in support of the Director of Communications.
Handled data entry, record keeping and the preparation of custom documents.

EDUCATION: American Institute for Paralegal Studies, Inc., Oakbrook Terrace, IL
Paralegal Certificate   Graduated 7/74

JANIS LESTER   *COMBINATION*

265 Spruce Drive #1B
Palatine, IL 60074   708/555-3098

EXPERIENCE:
- Proven ability to manage projects and create a solid rapport with clients in fast-paced, stressful environments.

- Staff training and supervision; develop strategies to determine and meet client's specific business needs.

- Plan and conduct presentations in a professional manner; create promotional materials and write customer correspondence; implement marketing strategies and provide full support for management and sales personnel.

- Experience in general bookkeeping, inventory control, purchasing and the preparation of status reports.

EMPLOYMENT: Culligan International, Northbrook, IL   6/90-Present
Meetings Coordinator - Office Services
Responsible for training and supervising two employees; coordinated numerous corporate conferences, business seminars, luncheons and employee recognition events. Simultaneously coordinate several functions daily to strict schedules and deadlines. Maintain accurate inventories of foods and beverages; work directly with vendors and suppliers for cost-effective purchasing.

* Act as liaison between management and staff at all levels.
* Featured in the corporate-wide newsletter under "Interesting People."

Merrill Lynch, Chicago, IL   5/87-5/90
Commodities Trading Assistant
Provided comprehensive market information and support to three account executives.
Performed daily research of Reuters, *The Wall Street Journal,* cash prices, and more than 50 markets and their respective options.
Communicated directly with the clientele regarding market shifts, strategies, and investment status.

Paine Webber, Chicago, IL   9/76-9/86
Account Executive / Trading Assistant
Developed a strong clientele and referral base in high-pressure business situations as a licensed Series 3 Broker.
Created and implemented individualized investment portfolios to meet client's specific goals; handled stock quotes, order placing and trade posting.
Designed and utilized a brochure explaining the concept of managed futures accounts.

* Acquired and managed several new, profitable accounts.
* Utilized the S&P 500 and hedged corporate stock portfolios estimated at $3 million.
* Successfully traded the commercial account of an internationally known food processor.
* Gained valuable experience as Trading Assistant to the former Chairman of the Chicago Board of Trade.

WCFL Radio, Chicago, IL
Contest Coordinator 1972-1976
Continuity Department 1967-1970
Organized promotional contests through interface with program directors, management, and various media representatives.
Handled cold-calling of major merchants for the acquisition of prices awarded to contest winners.

* Performed writing of creative copy used on this and other stations.
* Acted as public liaison responsible for written and oral communications; coordinated all "live" copy announced on the air by disk jockeys.
* Authored news stories and gained experience in newsroom operations.

EDUCATION: University of Iowa, Iowa City, IA 1971
B.A. Degree: English   Emphasis: Journalism

Additional training through the Chicago Board of Trade:
Introduction to Commodity Trading, 1978
Economic Factors of the Financial Instruments Markets, 1978
Economic Factors of the Market Place, 1978

The Chicago Mercantile Exchange:
Completed a Seminar on Options Trading, 1982

GARY S. KISIAN   *COMBINATION*

332 Atlantic Ave. #D
Hoffman Estates, IL 60194   708/555-6155

OBJECTIVE:	**Management / Training**
	A position where proven communication skills would be utilized.
EXPERIENCE:	■ More than six years combined experience in staff training and supervision, including full responsibility for program development and implementation.
	■ Familiar with DOS, Lotus 1-2-3, PageMaker, Excel, Macintosh and various Microsoft systems.
	■ Specialize in teaching professional customer service and communication techniques.

EMPLOYMENT: CPA Information Services, Chicago, IL   11/85-Present
Customer Service Trainer/Consultant   11/89-Present
Responsible for creating several unique customer service training manuals to meet specific department needs.
Plan and conduct monthly training sessions to improve customer service skills of individual representatives; provide feedback on strengths and weaknesses.
* Supervise bi-monthly feedback sessions with each department manager designed to improve worker morale and production.

Program Developer   3/90-11/89
Utilized Lotus to develop and administered the firm's Client Certification Exam.
Created a company reference module for all new employees.

Customer Service Manager   11/87-3/90
Acted as Operations Manager, consecutively, for four customer service divisions.
Responsible for troubleshooting with supervisors and claims managers from the nation's top 20 insurance companies.
* Hired, trained and monitored the performance of each Customer Service Representative.
* Managed budgets, payroll and bonus plans.

Customer Service Supervisor / Trainer   11/85-10/87
Supervised 12 employees and all department activities.
Gained excellent experience in problem solving with numerous insurance companies.

EDUCATION: Loyola University of Chicago, Chicago, IL
Bachelor of Science Degree   June, 1984
Major: Psychology   Minor: Communications

Dale Carnegie Course, Chicago, IL
Courses included Dealing with Difficult People, Operations Management and How to be an Effective Supervisor.

LISA M. EARNEST *COMBINATION / COLLEGE GRADUATE*

806 S. 63rd Avenue
Hickory Hills, IL 60457
708/555-3390: Permanent Address

920 Greenbrier
DeKalb, IL 60115
Until May 1991: 815/555-3401

OBJECTIVE:	A position where professional communication and organizational skills would be utilized and which offers the potential for career advancement.
EXPERIENCE:	■ Proven abilities in direct customer service, sales, writing and speech communications; experience in multi-media advertising, including ad design and the purchase of print and radio air time.
	■ Handle comprehensive research and report writing using WordStar, as well as data entry / retrieval on various computer systems.
	■ Train and supervise personnel; organize special events and conduct speeches & presentations in a professional manner.

EDUCATION: Northern Illinois University, DeKalb, IL
B.A. Degree   Graduated May, 1991
Major: Corporate Communications   Major GPA: 3.18/4.0

* Self-funded 100 percent of college costs.
* As Executive Board Member of Alpha Sigma Alpha Sorority, acted as Foods Chairman and managed a $16,000 budget; supervised a cook and waiters. As Assistant Social Chairman, planned numerous dances and social events.
* Advertising Chairman for NIU Springfest. Purchased ad space and successfully managed a multi-media advertising budget.
* Assistant Advertising Representative, The Northern Star Newspaper. Communicated with customers and provided creative input on ad design. Reviewed ads via phone and ensured their prompt, accurate placement.
* Teaching Assistant for a course entitled Exceptional Persons in Society. Involved in stimulating group discussions, grading papers and testing.
* Teacher's Assistant for a Communications Class; involved in program production and marketing.
* International Studies in Japan, Fall 1990. Completed several courses including East Asian Studies at Kansai Gaidai University, Hirakata City. Gained experience in Japanese language and culture.

EMPLOYMENT: Limited Express, Chicago Ridge, IL   Summers & Breaks, 1986-1991
Sales Associate
Responsible for direct customer service and sales, as well as merchandising and the set-up of retail displays.
Maintained accurate inventories and consistently met sales goals.
Involved in special promotions and the opening of two new stores.
* Two-time employee of the week.

HARRY LEWIS JR.   *CHRONOLOGICAL*

634 Chestnut Court   Buffalo Grove, IL 60089   708/555-0426

OBJECTIVE: A Sales career which offers the potential for professional advancement.

EMPLOYMENT: **Personal Attendant**   School Breaks, 1987-Present
<u>Jack Liver & Associates,</u> Palatine, IL
Act as corporate liaison and PR representative to key clientele and high-ranking corporate officials.
Provided entertainment and transportation.
Responsible for a full range of office and personnel functions.

Free-lance Painter   School Breaks, 1985-1988
Lawrence, KS
Determined and met customer's specific needs and painted residential and commercial properties.

Salesman/Installer   1988-Present
<u>Superdecks, Inc.,</u> Chicago, IL
Installed custom patio decks for a wide range of customers.
Presented written proposals, job estimates, and product benefits.

* Developed an extensive referral business through personalized communications.
* Hired, trained and supervised work crews and subcontractors.

EDUCATION: **Bachelor of Arts Degree**   May, 1989
<u>The University of Kansas</u>
Major: Economics
Completed extensive course work in History, Political Science and English
GPA: 3.3/4.0

* Honor Roll Student, four times.
* Financed 100 percent of college costs through employment and acquisition of student loans.
* Promoted and organized intramural activities for dormitory floor.

PERSONAL: Enjoy Golf, Softball, Music, and Reading.
Willing to travel or relocate.

CHARLES M. HAROLD *COMBINATION*

5412 Inland Drive #3B
Wheeling, IL 60090 708/555-1463

OBJECTIVE: Chemistry -- A position where diverse education and experience would be utilized.

EXPERIENCE:
- More than nine years of combined experience in laboratory procedures, product testing/inspection, quality control and customer relations.

- Comprehensive training in system design and development; handle in-depth research and produce written and oral reports in a professional manner.

- Familiar with Fortran, BASIC and various word processors.

EMPLOYMENT: Asbestos Control, Inc., Arlington Heights, IL Summers, 1985-1989 and 1990-Present
Certified Asbestos Abatement Workman
Responsible for asbestos removal from commercial and residential structures.
* Successfully trained and supervised abatement crews.

Bartlett Manufacturing, Elk Grove Village, IL 4/82-4/86
Promoted to the following positions, most recent first:
Assistant to Production Supervisor
Conducted tests on wastewater chemistry and worked directly with management in water quality maintenance/improvement.
Responsible for the collection, storage, and disposal of various hazardous wastes.
Quality Control Representative
Performed extensive laboratory testing of plating bath fluids.
Tested and maintained the quality of finished circuit boards.

Allis Chalmers Corp. Batavia, IL 6/78-1/82
Quality Control / Customer Service Representative
Communicated with dealers and answered questions on part specifications and use.
Maintained excellent quality of finished parts.

Fermilab, Batavia, IL 3/77-2/78
Technician
Assembled superconductor magnet systems as R&D Group Member.
Involved in Cryostat Group Activities and magnet testing.

Steel Trading, Aurora, IL 2/76-11/76
Shipping / Material Handling Foreman
Supervised four employees in shipping/receiving and inventory control.

EDUCATION: University of Illinois, Urbana, IL Graduated 12/89
B.S. Degree, Chemistry Minor: Chemical Engineer
Courses involved the design of a distillation column, a separation process using heat transfer principles and a chemical separation plant, including the calculation of budgets and related economics.
Member: AICHE 1986-1988 and Delta Phi Fraternity

JUDY ROSEALL　　　　　　　　　　　　　　　　　　　　　　　　　　*COMBINATION*

6804 East Old Willow Road
Prospect Heights, IL 60070　　　　　　　　　　　　　　　　　　　708/555-6874

OBJECTIVE:	**Floral Design Expeditor** A position where leadership and creative talents would be utilized.
EXPERIENCE:	■ More than four years in the creative design and sale of floral arrangements for weddings, ceremonies and special events. ■ Experience in job scheduling, order expediting and cost effective purchasing. ■ Staff training and supervision in customer service, inventory control, merchandising and the substitution of flowers for special arrangements.
EMPLOYMENT:	Jewel Foods, Lake Zurich, IL　　　　　　　　　　　　　　　12/85-Present **Floral Clerk** In charge of the production and expediting of large and small floral arrangements for weddings and other occasions. - Handle stock ordering; assist in merchandising and inventory control. - Organize sales and payroll data. - Regularly attend major design shows. Silk Green House, Evanston, IL　　　　　　　　　　Part-Time, 8/90-Present **Floral Clerk** Responsible for direct customer service and sales to a wide range of clientele. Set up retail displays; handle merchandising and stocking; assist in inventory control. Sun Garden Floral Shop, Evanston, IL　　　　　　　　　　　　　　　1985 **Floral Clerk** Designed floral arrangements and communicated with customers in a professional manner. Colette's Flower Shop, Winnetka, IL　　　　　　　　　　　　　　　1985 **Floral Clerk**
EDUCATION:	American Floral Art School, Chicago, IL **Floral Design** courses included experience in labor management, cost analyses, design planning/estimating, purchasing, cost effectiveness and flower substitutions. The College of Lake County, Grayslake, IL Completed courses in Basic Ornamental Horticulture

ANTHONY VARGOS   *FUNCTIONAL*

18 Windbrook Drive #101
Buffalo Grove, IL 60089   708/555-0372

OBJECTIVE: Genetic Engineering
A position where diverse technical skills would be utilized.

EXPERIENCE:
- Experience in DNA cloning and subcloning using plasmid vectors; techniques include sterile handling of bacterial cultures, plasmid DNA purification and band separations by ultra centrifugation with CsCl gradient.

- Skilled in restriction enzyme splicing and separation of different size fragments on agarose gel electrophoresis, as well as DNA ligation and transformation into competent bacterial cells.

- Perform Sanger method DNA sequencing; experience in projects involving enzyme kinetics, protein purification/characterization and quantitative/qualitative chemistry.

- Analytical chemistry experience includes working with fat and carbohydrate substitutes; conduct viscosity analyses using modern viscometers.

- Determine particle sizes and counts; utilize Coulter multi-sizing instruments; familiar with titrations, microscopy and ion conductivity.

EMPLOYMENT: NutraSweet, Mt. Prospect, IL   8/90-Present

Research Technologist - subcontractor basis
Involved in projects related to the development of Simplesse and various carbohydrates.
Configure and perform a wide range of laboratory tests.

EDUCATION: Western Illinois University, Macomb, IL
Master's Degree   1989-Present
Completed all coursework towards Master's Degree in May, 1990. Currently completing a thesis entitled "Genetic processing of T-DNA in agrobacteria."

Bachelor's Degree - Chemistry   1986-1988
Emphasis in Biochemistry; minor: Microbiology.

Elgin Community College, Elgin, IL
Completed general courses   1984-1986

Nursing School Graduate   1981
High School Graduate   1979

MARY T. STARR COMBINATION

110 Sunnyside Beach Drive
McHenry, IL 60050   815/555-7297

OBJECTIVE: A position utilizing a full range of talents in Business Administration, Communications, and Human Relations.

EXPERIENCE:
- Proficient in training, lecturing, and the development of teaching materials; plan and conduct written and oral presentations in a professional manner.

- Proven abilities in sales, marketing, and business policy development; administer budgets and payroll; procure capital equipment and maintain accurate inventories.

- Hire, train and supervise professional staff; experienced in personnel administration and the planning/implementation of special projects and events.

EMPLOYMENT: Northern Illinois Country Day School, McHenry, IL   1983-Present
Manager / Owner
Responsible for all operations at this preschool and kindergarten facility, including promotions, sales, marketing, and budget coordination.
* Successfully determined all aspects of the set-up and maintenance of this growing business, including the hiring and supervision of all teaching staff.

St. Priscilla School, Chicago, IL   1980-1983
Principal
In charge of all aspects of management for 37 teachers, as well as the development of cost-effective policies and school procedures.
* Managed budgets and payroll as member of the Policy Committee Board.
* Developed and executed curricula for virtually all general subjects.
* Personally opened student math, reading, and psychological testing centers.

Transfiguration Elementary School, Wauconda, IL   1971-1980
Principal
Supervised 14 teachers, including hiring, performance review, and termination.
* Created the science department and acquired all necessary capital equipment.
* Opened a new computer center, involving the cost-effective sourcing and purchasing of all computers and related peripherals.

Prior Experience:
More than ten year's experience teaching in various Catholic Schools. Taught grades 3 and 5 general studies; taught Science and History at the Jr. High School level.

EDUCATION: DePaul University, Chicago, IL
M.Ed. Degree: Emphasis: Administration and Supervision.

Mundelein College, Chicago, IL
B.A. Degree: Education

1228 Fall Court
Schaumburg, IL 60193

ROBERT L. SAMPLE

MANAGEMENT / COMBINATION

708/555-2160

MANAGEMENT / SALES & ENGINEERING

EXPERIENCE:
- Management experience (sales & engineering) includes divisional product responsibility for displays and custom/semi-custom I.C.s. This involves marketing, profitability and quality control.

- Maintain excellent relationships with key managers and engineers at the world's largest electronics and automotive firms.

- Skilled in budget planning, sales forecasting, and competitive analysis; experience in tactical marketing and new product introduction.

- Train and supervise staff in major account acquisition and development; proven ability to optimize company distribution and support activities.

- Experience in Japanese and Matrix management methods; well-versed in a variety of electronics manufacturing environments and techniques.

TECHNICAL PROFILE:

Skilled in digital and analog design; 4, 8, & 16 bit microprocessor systems development; minicomputer interface/system design, servo-hydraulic devices, machine code through Fortran languages; proficient in LCD and TFT display development.

Product design expertise in various automotive electronic systems: engine controls, instrumentation, and charging systems. Experience with CPU subsystems and LSI testers, LSI architecture development and failure analysis.

EMPLOYMENT:

<u>Sony Corporation,</u> Chicago, IL   1988-Present
Division Engineering Manager - Electronic Display Division
Manage up to 17 engineer/technical sales staff & managers and all aspects of tactical marketing and application engineering.
Created a special task force and regained this division's market position.
Successfully realigned market focus, narrowed customer base and focused on major OEMs.
* Achieved 60 percent budget growth for this division over three years.
* Planned and implemented current U.S. sales and engineering structures.
* Created a Q.C. tracking and early warning system.
* Developed a technical service center for this division.
* Initiated the use of satellites for worldwide design center communications.

<u>Hitachi Semiconductor Division Responsibilities:</u>
National Application Engineering Manager - San Jose, CA   1986-1988
Directed tactical field activity for this division's strategic account base.
Acted as liaison to a Japan-based design center.
Involved in LSI Architectural development for a 4 & 8 bit product family.
* Custom/semi-custom LSI budget of $8 M/month.
* Developed a national engineering program and centralized management functions.
* Created a technical training program and M.B.O. -- career development programs.
* Developed a strategic business plan for a 16 bit microfamily through beta level.

Regional Engineering Manager - Dearborn, MI   1985-1986
Responsible for all aspects of regional sales engineering, including objectives, budgets, personnel planning, bonus structures and territory assignments.
* Established strategies for a custom LSI growth plan and achieved budget expansion from $2.5 M to $3.5 M/month.

Application Engineering Specialist - Dearborn, MI   1984-1985
Designated microprocessor application specialist to GM, Ford, and Chrysler Corporation.

Ford Motor Company, Electronics Division, Dearborn, MI   1981-1984
Product Design Engineer - Electronic Instrumentation
Acted as project engineer/design engineer on systems which included:
* Thunderbird, 1983: electronic instrument cluster, designed & released.
* Grand Marquis, 1984: electronic instrument cluster, designed & released.
* Lincoln Town Car, 1984: electron fuel gauge/trip computer, designed & released.
* Aerostar Van, 1985: electronic instrument cluster, systems design.

Senior Test Engineer - Electronic Systems Engineering   1978-1981
Responsibilities included failure analysis (LSI) engineering and the development of in-house semiconductor analysis expertise. Utilized electron microscopy, computer modeling and chemical analyses.
Directed a design team responsible for creating in-house, micro-based automation.
Planned and implemented an in-house LSI automatic testing facility; determined specifications and procurement procedures.

Product Development Engineer - Elect. Engine Controls, Power Train Div.   1976-1978
Directed a team designing all CPU testing facilities.
* Member of the CPU architecture design team for 1980 electronic engine control.
* Developed an automated drive simulation system for a new approach to electronic engine development. This allowed full simulation of an electronic drive sequence.

System Design Engineer   1972-1976
Accepted full responsibility for the design of computerized testing facilities utilizing minicomputers, microprocessors, custom interfaces and analog/digital circuitry.
Designed servo systems and hydraulic systems as well as:
* A dynamometer/parametric alternator system.
* An automated system for characterizing digital clock performance.
* The industry's first fully automated shock absorber characterizer.
* An automated electronic ignition/distributor emission certification system.

EDUCATION: Oklahoma State University, Stillwater, OK
B.S. Electronic Engineering   1972
Saint Pat's Salute Award -- Leadership and Scholarship; Tau Iota Epsilon Award; Honorable Mention: Who's Who on American College Campuses.
Member: SAE, IEEE; President of S.E.E.T. and Secretary of the Engineering Student Council.

DANIEL D. SHARK *EXECUTIVE / COMBINATION*

120 Field Drive
Glendale Heights, IL 60139   708/555-3729

EXPERIENCE:
- Skilled in coordinating sales, marketing and distribution networks in worldwide markets; manage strategic planning and competitive analyses.

- Organize advertising, promotions and public relations activities; plan and conduct technical and sales presentations at meetings, conventions and trade shows with professional communication skills.

- Hire, train and supervise laboratory/technical staff, sales teams and operations management at virtually all levels of experience.

- Proven ability to convert profit losing operations to profit gainers through detailed planning and staff/management motivation.

- Plan and implement budgets and long & short-term business programs; handle comprehensive financial analysis, forecasting, modeling and spreadsheet development.

- Executive-level talents in product development/introduction, international marketing and business administration, including full responsibility for P&L and new ventures.

CAREER BACKGROUND: CDG Food Corporation, Elmsford, NY   5/88-Present

Vice President / General Manager
In charge of U.S. business activities including primary responsibility for marketing and business development for this firm specializing in creating, distributing and marketing food ingredients worldwide; sales exceed $20 mm.

Report directly to president/owner and coordinate the cost-effective development of products including a natural MSG replacement, a line of amino acids and natural butyric acids and their related processes.

-- Directly involved in hiring and training laboratory, administrative, accounting and research personnel.
-- Responsible for five employees and all aspects of management for a professional sales and distribution network.
-- Supervise a private labeling program for all products and processes which has increased international awareness of virtually all PTX endeavors.
-- Increased baking industry market share for Cultured Whey products from 40 percent to 65 percent.

-- Improved market awareness and exposure for PTX through regular involvement in a variety of trade advertising programs and conventions, including the Institute of Food Technology.

Pennant Products, Inc. Rochester, NY   3/87-5/88
Currently a division of Van den Bergh Foods Company.

Divisional Sales Manager
Personally directed marketing and sales functions for bakery products, mixes and frozen/prepared items in a 17-state region.
Hired, trained and supervised four territory managers and planned & implemented all marketing programs through interface with company president.

-- Acquired and managed several national accounts.
-- Developed and maintained all product distribution channels within the division.
-- Established a national service relationship with such key accounts as Super Valu, Scribners, American Fruit, Nash Finch, Federated Foods and Sysco.
-- Responsible for creating Pennant's first sales, distribution and service programs in Wisconsin, Minnesota, Iowa and Nebraska.

New Zealand Milk Products/N.Z. Farms, Inc. Petaluma, CA   7/85-11/86

General Manager
Involved in the startup and operation of this firm which packaged, marketed and sold specialty cheese products to retail accounts.
Hired and directed key managers for production, marketing, sales, advertising, retail promotion and general business administration.

-- Created detailed short and long-range business and marketing plans.
-- Established a broker network and organized distribution of imported New Zealand Cheeses throughout seven west-coast states.
-- Successfully positioned New Zealand Milk Products firmly in profitable retail & food service markets.

Quali Tech, Inc., Chaska, MN   9/83-3/85

General Manager / National Sales Manager, Food Products Division
Developed all sales and marketing programs for this marketing and manufacturing group producing food ingredients.
Represented and marketed to industrial food manufacturers in the U.S. and Canada.

-- NOTE: This division was formed following the purchase of the food ingredient division of the Peavey Company (listed below).
-- As former Division Manager with Peavey, managed existing business and integrated totally new health food products and marketing programs.
-- Introduced & marketed five new health foods and an industrial food ingredient.

Peavey Company, Chaska, MN 6/68-9/83
Merged with ConAgra, 1981

Venture Manager / General Manager, Food Ingredient Division 12/77-9/83
In charge of all aspects of management and procedure development for this independent food ingredient production and sales firm entitled *Nugget Venture* within Peavey Company.
Supervised national promotions and hired/trained all staff, 25 percent of whom were promoted.

- -- Assisted in the sale of *Nugget Venture* to Quali Tech, Inc.
- -- Directed solid sales growth of 22 percent annually, with net profits exceeding 15 percent.
- -- *Nugget Venture* gained recognition throughout the industry for its many innovations and pilot programs, as well as process engineering and new product development.
- -- Instrumental in the turnaround of this division from a profit loser to Peavey's highest profit gainer.

Territory Manager, Bakery Flour Sales, Allentown, PA 7/69-12/77
Directed all contract sales in the Midwest and East coast, including contract acquisition and scheduling for bakery flours, mixes and institutional products.

- -- Attained or exceeded sales goals for all product lines each year and increased territories three-fold.
- -- Responsible for more than 20 percent of total company mix sales.
- -- Achieved regular sales increases of 10 percent to 30 percent.

Divisional Sales Assistant, Scarsdale, NY 4/69-6/69
Management Trainee, Minneapolis, MN 6/68-3/69

PROFESSIONAL MEMBERSHIPS: Institute of Food Technologies
American Association of Cereal Chemists

EDUCATION: University of Southern Minnesota, Mankato, MN
B.S. Degree -- Business Administration/Economics Graduated 1968

MILITARY: U.S. Air Force, San Antonio, TX 1963-1966
Kelly Air Force Base
Sergeant: Top Secret Clearance

PERSONAL: Excellent health.
Willing to travel or relocate, excellent references available upon request.

CONTESSA M. BERGER   *COMBINATION*

38 Chelsea Drive
Bartlett, IL 60103   708/555-0160

OBJECTIVE: **Teacher**
                       A position in English or Social Studies at the High School or Jr. High School level.

EXPERIENCE: *   Certified in grades 6-12 English and Social Studies; experience in cooperative learning, lecturing, discussion and group management.

                       *   Plan and implement daily lessons using various study guides and audio/visual materials.

                       *   Experience in teaching narrative, expository, descriptive and creative writing with an emphasis on style.

                       *   Background in class instruction using WordStar and Macintosh computers.

                       *   Enjoy coaching cross-country and track; interested in leading student writing and reading clubs.

TRAINING: **Student Teacher**   8/90-12/90
                       Batavia High School, Batavia, IL
                       Responsible for teaching two courses in American Literature, two courses in Regular English, and a course in Basic English.

                       Taught sophomores, juniors, and seniors; organized discussion groups and evaluated individual performance.
                       Topics included novels and short stories by authors such as Poe, Emerson, Thoreau, Cooper, Irving, Golding and Hawthorne.

                       *   Taught English basics to a Polish immigrant, considered a zero English-speaking student.

EDUCATION: Northern Illinois University, DeKalb, IL   5/91
                       B.A. Degree
                       Major: English   Minor: History
                       *   Dean's List, three semesters

PRIOR
EXPERIENCE: **Receptionist**, Summer, 1987
                       Responsibilities included typing, telephone answering and general office work.
                       Employed in various waitress and retail positions throughout college.

PERSONAL: Willing to travel or relocate.
                       Sierra Club Member and Environmentalist.
                       Enjoy reading, jogging, and regular exercise.

MICHAEL E. ABBOT
5292 Shadow Bend Drive
Wheeling, IL 60090
708/555-6888

COMBINATION

SALES / SALES MANAGEMENT

EXPERIENCE

- More than 17 years in sales and sales management, including success with leading manufacturing firms in major metropolitan markets.

- Handle comprehensive research and competitive analysis for the implementation of marketing strategies.

- Assist in staff training and supervision with excellent communication skills; develop a strong "team" atmosphere among sales reps and support personnel.

- Determine and meet client's specific business needs; plan and conduct sales presentations with key clientele in a personalized, professional manner.

- Demonstrated success in creating long-term business partnerships through effective organization.

EMPLOYMENT

King Manufacturing, Manhattan, NY   1986-Present
Midwest District Sales Manager   1989-Present
Responsible for sales to mass merchants for this home textile marketer which has a national client base generating $100 million annually. Work directly with merchants at major chains, department stores, supermarkets and drug stores.

Manage budgets, determine sales quotas and penetration strategies, and monitor co-op advertising efforts on a regular basis. Effectively train and supervise a broker sales force and various company representatives.

* Personally handle major accounts including Venture, Walgreens, Kohls, Osco Drug, Pamida, Shopko, Meijers and Cotter & Company,
* Increased sales from $800,000 to $3.5 million, 1986-Present.
* Established productive relationships with major accounts resulting in a dramatic rebound in the Midwest. Hired and trained a new sales representative for Program Selling in Indianapolis. This resulted in a dramatic sales increase for a previously dormant territory.
* Promoted to this position from **Senior Midwest Account Executive**, 1986-1989.

The Bali Company, A division of Sara Lee, Winston-Salem, NC   1984-1986
Chicago Regional Sales Manager   1985-1986
Management duties included the development of buying plans and sales forecasts for this manufacturer of intimate apparel.
Handled key accounts and worked directly with senior store management.

* Trained and supervised four sales associates & field merchandisers working with major accounts such as Marshall Fields, Carson Pirie Scott and other retailers.

Key Account Sales Representative - Chicago / Milwaukee   1984-1985
Responsible for key account sales to major department stores.
Maintained direct communication with buying staff and senior store management regarding volume and profitability.
Trained and supervised three sales associates.

Patrick H. Joyce & Associates, Des Plaines, IL   1983-1984
Account Executive
Called directly on national advertisers to plan and implement marketing and communication programs.
Worked primarily with point-of-purchase displays and package designs, as well as sales promotions and related materials.

Maidenform, Inc. New York, NY   1981-1983
Key Account Sales Representative - Chicago / Milwaukee
Responsible for the sale of branded product lines to major department stores, as well as specialty and military accounts. Presented national promotions for new products and programs.

Developed/implemented effective buying plans and generated monthly reorders.
Supervised one merchandiser and maintained excellent communications with key accounts.

* Instrumental in launching marketing campaigns which increased sales and service demands.
* Acted as liaison between company and accounts to provide timely information, expedite service and resolve conflicts.
* Increased sales volume 12 percent, 1981-1983.

Kayser-Roth Intimate Apparel Company, Inc. New York, NY   1973-1981
Field Sales Representative
Conducted high-volume sales to major department stores, as well as military and specialty accounts.
Involved in all phases of direct sales, including program development, inventory control and customer relations.

* Recognized for excellent sales performance.
* Increased sales volume in last assigned territory by $315,000.

EDUCATION

Northeastern University, Boston, MA
Bachelor of Arts Degree / Marketing   1973

Xerox Corporation
Completed Selling Skills II Course

PERSONAL

Willing to travel extensively; references available upon request.

KATY J. COSENTINO

CHRONOLOGICAL With Brief Summaries

516 North West Avenue
Elmhurst, IL 60126

708/555-5154

GENERAL PSYCHOLOGY:

- Experience in assessment and therapy for groups, individuals, families, children and adolescents.

HUMAN RESOURCES:

- Extensive background in employee counseling and the development and documentation of plant safety and administrative programs.

EXPERIENCE:

M&M / SNICKERS, Chicago, IL 1974-Present
Special Projects Clerk, Technical Section 1986-Present
Responsibilities include editing and publishing the *Safety Newsletter* for all employees.
Design incentive programs to improve plant safety.
Process Workmen's Compensation claims.
Maintain all records and financial reports related to special projects and arrange activities for associates.

- Member of Safety Promotions Committee
- Serve on Management Safety Committee

Special Projects Clerk, R & D Section 1985-1986
Directly involved in writing and producing a Good Manufacturing Practices Handbook, including the FDA's requirements for good manufacturing practices and organization standards. This is currently being distributed.
Assisted in the installation of a new chocolate plant in the facility.
Visited manufacturing plants in England, and coordinated support for British employees visiting the Chicago plant. Arranged worker accommodations, as well as traveler's checks, access to AT&T charge cards, and sightseeing.
Maintained cash receipts, financial records and clerical support.
Worked with 5-8 employees and helped to relieve tension and stress related to various projects.

- Sampled products on a random basis to maintain quality to company standards.
- Conducted training programs for OSHA.
- Developed and presented a system to prepare employees for a major test.

Human Resources Representative 1974-1985
Conducted intervention counseling of employees with both medical and personal problems; and referred them to appropriate doctors or other professionals as needed.
Communicated directly with employees regarding benefits, workers' compensation, accident & health benefits and long term disability benefits.
Arranged activities for associates, including dances and dinners.
Screened applications, conducted interviews and recruited for various positions.

- Assisted in organizing a program for English as a second language.
- Explored options in developing an illiteracy program.
- Involved in counseling associates of lost family members.
- Assisted employees with alcohol-related problems received necessary counseling and benefits.

EDUCATION:

Forest Institute, IL
Currently working toward **MS Degree** in Psychology
Expected graduation: September, 1991

National College of Education, Lombard, IL
MA Degree, Management and Human Resource Development, June 1985

Rosary College, River Forest, IL
BA Degree, Psychology, May 1982

Additional coursework, 1986-Present:
- Theories of Personality
- Management of Addiction Treatment Programs
- Human Development 1 and Personal & Prof. Development 1
- Human Development 2 and Personal & Prof. Development 2

- Thinking, Motivation Emotion and Personal & Prof. Development 3
- Sexual Abuse
- Biological Bases 1 and 3
- Winter 1988 Bio bases of human behavior 2 and 1: Perception and Maturation

- Psychopathology 3 and psych. intervention 3
- Clinical Skills 1
- Psychopathology and Psych. Assessment 1
- Psych Assessment 2 and Psych. Intervention 2
- Social Psychology and Psych. Assessment 3

- Research Design & Methods 1: Basic Statistics and Psych. Intervention 1
- Research Design & Methods 2: Advanced Stats. and Psychopathology 2
- Research Design & Methods 3: Advance Stats completed 6/19/90

923 West Leland
Chicago, IL 60630

NICOLI PACINO

COMBINATION

312/555-8736

OBJECTIVE: A position in Hotel/Restaurant Food & Beverage Management.

EXPERIENCE:
- More than eight years combined experience in hotel/restaurant food service, including full responsibility for staff hiring, training, and supervision.
- Proven abilities in marketing, promotions, labor/product cost control and effective customer service; organize kitchens and sanitation procedures.
- Excellent communication skills; maintain positive relations with staff and customers in high-volume operations.

EMPLOYMENT:

Days Inn, Gurnee, IL   10/90-Present
Assistant Restaurant Manager
Responsible for training and supervising up to six employees per shift.
Assist the general manager in food & beverage inventory/cost control and purchasing.

Sheraton North Shore Inn, Northbrook, IL   4/90-10/90
Assistant Restaurant Manager
In charge of all front-of-house operations, including training and supervision of up to ten employees.
Work with F&B director in the development of theme buffets for breakfast, lunch and Friday nights.
- Involved in room service operations and work related to the Garden Grille and two lounges.
- Assisted F&B director in creating a new wine list and hiring new employees.

McCormick Center Hotel, Chicago, IL   8/89-4/90
Waiter
Responsible for professional customer service; primarily served convention guests at Latrec's high-volume restaurant and lounge.

1-2-3 Club, Chicago, IL   10/87-7/89
Bartender
Reported directly to owner and assisted in creative advertising, special events planning and inventory control; analyzed competitor's operations.

Burger America, Madison, WI   1/87-9/87
Co-Manager
Trained/supervised up to 12 employees in food preparation and customer service.
Organized special promotions with local high school and softball teams.

EDUCATION: Madison Area Technical College Madison, WI   1984-1986
Completed courses in the Hotel/Restaurant Management Program.

CHRONOLOGICAL / NEW GRADUATE

RICHARD A. INGLE

Until May 20, 1991:
818-D Greenbrier Road
DeKalb, IL 60115
815/555-3166

After May 20, 1991:
331 S. Salem Drive
Schaumburg, IL 60193
708/555-1523

OBJECTIVE: **Mechanical Engineering:** A position utilizing skills in computer aided design.

EDUCATION: Northern Illinois University, DeKalb, IL
B.S. Degree: College of Engineering   Expected Graduation: May, 1991
Major: Mechanical Engineering   Minor: Mathematics
Major GPA: 3.04/4.0; Cumulative GPA: 3.00/4.00

Courses included:
- Engineering Graphics with Autocad
- Statics, Dynamics and Fluids
- Thermodynamics and Heat Transfer

Assistant Instructor / President
NIU Tae Kwon Do Club
Train and supervise two classes, including student motivation and performance evaluation.

Continental Cablevision, Palatine, IL
Directly involved in the production of special television programs.

EXPERIENCE: Blackie's Plastic Mold Co., Addison, IL
Summer Internship   1989-1990
Responsible for the use and maintenance of lathes, mills, drill presses, grinders, band saws and various hand tools.
Involved in the production of steel and aluminum molds, including drilling and polishing of finished products.

Gardner Tree and Landscaping, Bensenville, IL
Supervisor   Summer, 1988
In charge of up to seven employees in various landscaping activities.
Ensured customer satisfaction and maintained all equipment on a regular basis.

Jiffy Lube, Oak Brook, IL
Technician   1985-1986

Red Cross Shoes, Schaumburg, IL
Stock Clerk   1984-1985
Updated and maintained accurate inventories.
Handled shipping, receiving and pricing of merchandise.

NAME

Address
City, State Zip Code
Phone Number

From GETTING HIRED IN THE '90s
(Condensed to one page)

ACHIEVEMENTS/AWARDS

Midwest Account Executive of year 1980 (Rookie Year)
Ranked in top five in nation 1980 - 1985 (125 offices)
Nominated producing manager of year 1981
Hall of Fame 1985
Awarded five National Pacesetter Trips
Authored book *GETTING HIRED IN THE '90s*

PROFESSIONAL EXPERIENCE

9/89 to Present

Company Name
Account Manager/Independent Contractor
Market employment services via telephone and client visits
Manage personnel functions for 50 clients
Assist in hiring, training and evaluating new employees
Recruit, interview and consult candidates regarding career moves

Highlights
- Increased office production and client base by 45 percent
- Helped create and implement client presentation and training materials

7/87 to 9/89

Company Name
6/88 - 9/89
General Manager
Developed corporate identity program for start-up operation including name, logo, marketing materials, training program and advertising
Complete autonomy for new division
Responsible for hiring, training and motivating staff of 12
Created on-premise division

EDUCATIONAL BACKGROUND

Name of University
Courses Studied or Major
Specialized Training
Real Estate 101
Tom Hopkins Sales Training
Zig Ziglar Seminar
Dale Carnegie
Computer Literate
IBM PC/Word Perfect 5.0

PAUL T. STONE

COMBINATION

167 N. Slusher
Grayslake, IL 60030

708/555-8807 Bus.
708/555-9040 Res.

OBJECTIVE: A position utilizing an extensive background in Distribution Management, Freight Routing and Warehousing.

EXPERIENCE:

- More than nine years of combined experience in management and distribution activities, including full responsibility for warehouse organizing, employee supervision and operational efficiency.

- Handle freight routing, traffic management and cost-effective rate negotiation with freight carriers; assist in budget development and procedure planning/updating.

- Experience in capital equipment purchasing; skilled in the set-up and maintenance of inventory control systems and computerized FI/FO operations.

- Hire, train and supervise warehouse and support personnel at virtually all levels of experience.

EMPLOYMENT: <u>Jones-Rakin, Inc.</u>, Midwest Distribution Center, Wheeling, IL   1981-Present

Distribution Supervisor   1984-Present
Responsible for all incoming and outgoing foreign and domestic shipments for this center, a division of the world's largest manufacturer and importer of gifts and specialty items.
Work directly with customs brokers; involved in cost-effective routing and trafficking on a daily basis.
Train and supervise 20 employees in shipping/receiving and distribution procedures, including hiring, performance review and termination.
Purchase forklifts, conveyors, shelving and general office equipment.

* Directly responsible for the set-up of a computerized product locator system, which involved detailed zoning of the entire warehouse. Location/movement of all stock is tracked and updated by computer every four hours.
* As Safety Officer, created a safety lottery with cash incentives for all employees, resulting in a 65 percent decrease in reportable accident claims.
* Directly involved in the layout and organizing of three major warehouses, including the implementation of construction specifications with contractors.
* Successfully completed three seminars sponsored by Dakin, Inc. and presented by National Seminars, Inc.:

  - How to Supervise People
  - How to Handle Difficult People
  - How to Get Things Done

PAUL T. STONE

Lead Position / Foreman 1982-1984
In charge of warehouse crews of up to 20 employees in order picking, truck loading/unloading and shipping.

General Warehouseman 1981-1982

The Interim, Bar & Restaurant, Glenview, IL 1975-1981
Manager
Trained and supervised cooks, bartenders and wait staff in all restaurant procedures. Responsible for purchasing all food, beverages and entertainment for this high-volume establishment.

* Maintained excellent quality of food and service.
* Involved in advertising, promotions and merchandising.

PRIOR EXPERIENCE: Harrah's Casino, Lake Tahoe, NV
Blackjack Dealer 1.5 Years

The Pizza Palace, Los Gatos, CA
Line Cook 8 Months

EDUCATION: St. Mary's College, Winona, MN
B.S. Degree -- Major: Political Science 1972
Major GPA: 3.0/4.0

Loyola Academy, Wilmette, IL
Graduate, College Preparatory School

MARY J. BARBARA   *COMBINATION*

340 Thunder Lane
Elgin, IL 60123   708/555-2807

OBJECTIVE: A position where proven Management and Supervisory skills would be utilized.

EXPERIENCE:
- More than six years in the cost-effective supervision of production activities, including full traffic management responsibilities.

- Handle employee hiring, training and supervision with solid communication and motivational skills; fluent in Spanish.

- Experience in shipping/receiving, parts requisitioning, inventory control and status reporting.

EMPLOYMENT: Round Bearing Company, Wheeling, IL   8/80-Present
Traffic Manager - Chain Division
Responsible for shipping and receiving of parts and supplies; handle rate negotiations with carriers and maintain accurate records of incoming shipments.
Train, supervise and review the performance of 14 employees in the assembly and cutting of virtually all types of chains.
Delegate and expedite all duties; provide leadership necessary to maintain strong worker morale and motivation.
Process worker time cards and payroll information on a regular basis.

* Successfully consolidated four divisions of Peer Bearing and reduced freight charges by 60 percent.
* Promoted to this position from Inventory Controller and Order Puller.

Zenith Corporation, Elk Grove, IL   1978-1980
Assembler
Responsible for production line assembly of television components.
Updated and maintained daily production status reports for management.

Motorola, Schaumburg, IL   1973-1977
Assembler
Assembled circuit boards on a busy production line.
Utilized test equipment including oscilloscopes and multimeters.

EDUCATION: Elgin Community College, Elgin, IL   1973
Successful completion of courses in Data Processing, Accounting and English.

High School Graduate   1972

KARIM K. JABAR

133 Florence Way
Glenview, IL 60025

COMBINATION

708/555-3570

OBJECTIVE:	An Accounting position where proven skills and attention to detail would be utilized.
EXPERIENCE:	▪ More than four years in general accounting, including full responsibility for accounts payable/receivable, journal entries and general ledger maintenance.
	▪ Familiar with Lotus 1-2-3, VisiCalc, COBOL, BASIC, and IBM PCs.
	▪ Design and analyze spreadsheets; process payrolls and reconcile portfolios; generate status reports and financial statements promptly and accurately.
	▪ Assist in staff hiring, training/supervision and employee relations.

EMPLOYMENT: Total Management, Inc., Deerfield, IL
Property Accountant 9/89-11/90
Responsible for accounts receivable, journal entries and financial statement preparation.
Created and distributed monthly variance reports for management.
Analyzed statements and disbursements; generated and reviewed monthly reports on receipts and disbursements for HUD.

* Reconciled final payroll & portfolios related to the management of 75 properties upon relocation of this company's accounting department to Seattle, Washington.

Legends, Chicago, IL
Accountant 5/89-7/89
Accepted this temporary position, involving the preparation of financial statements, journal entries and AP/AR.

Harry Caray's, Chicago, IL
Accountant 1/88-12/88
Processed all invoices, paid vendors and issued checks for various payments.
Responsible AP/AR, JEs and financial statements.

Carmen's Pizzeria, Chicago, IL
Coordinator of Deliveries 10/86-1/88
Hired, trained and supervised 12 employees in pizza delivery and sales.
Monitored cash flows and handled all general bookkeeping related to deliveries.

EDUCATION: Roosevelt University, Chicago, IL
B.S.B.A. Degree - Accounting Major May, 1988
Courses included Finance, Management and Lotus 1-2-3.

JACK C. MANNING

COMBINATION

199 Hillside Road
Northbrook, IL 60062

708/555-4752

SALES / MANAGEMENT

EXPERIENCE:
- Proven abilities in project management and professional client relations, including full profit/loss responsibilities.

- Account prospecting, acquisition and management; experience in job costing and full customer service and support.

- Staff training and supervision in sales and product installations.

- Project planning and sales forecasting; experience in computerized account tracking and inventory control.

EMPLOYMENT: <u>Unique Indoor Comfort, Inc.</u>, Kenilworth, IL   1971-9/91

Inventory Foreman & Service Dispatcher   1990-9/91
Performed sales, customer service and sales support for this major manufacturer of Space-Pak, a high-quality, specialty central air conditioning system.
Sales averaged $12,000 each.
Assisted in job pricing and the sale/installation of heating systems, attic fans, humidifiers and electrical systems.
Responsible for training, supervising and assigning professional installation crews.

- Maintained an accurate inventory of parts and tracked/updated accounts on an HP 3000 mainframe computer.
- Managed and improved virtually all warehouse operations.

Inventory Foreman and Installer   Seven months, 1990

Head Mechanic   1973-1990
Trained and supervised more than 30 employees in product installation, sales and service, four of whom were promoted to management.

- Successfully installed more than 1,000 central systems and achieved this company's highest profit margin for one year: 26 percent.
- Directly involved in producing a slide presentation currently in use by marketing personnel.
- Completed company-sponsored classes entitled Manager's Guide to Human Behavior and Communication Skills at Elmhurst College.

Sales Representative   1971-1973
Responsible for lead prospecting, cold calling and account acquisition & management.
Sold complete systems throughout the Chicagoland area.

Orrington Hotel, Evanston, IL   1968-1971
Food Service Manager
Trained and supervised 30 employees in wait and bus activities.
Managed all front-of-house activities for three dining rooms and a banquet room with facilities for 500.

* Ensured customer satisfaction and top quality of all services.
* Promoted to this position from Desk Clerk.

Harris Trust and Savings, Money Transfer Division, Chicago, IL   1967-1968
Corporate Cashier
Responsible for the prompt, accurate transfer of millions of dollars between banks and corporations on a daily basis.

Abbott Metals, Chicago, IL   1966-1967
Manufacturer's Representative
Accurately determined and met client's needs in high-volume sales of steel to major corporate accounts; planned and conducted sales presentations to senior-level clientele.
Prospected and acquired numerous accounts.
Assisted in shipping and material routing as needed.

* Achieved a major sale of more than 33 tons of steel from England to Gary, Indiana.

EDUCATION: Successful completion of college classes in Business and Liberal Arts.
High School Graduate.

MILITARY: United States Marines, San Diego, Virginia, and Sea Duty
Staff Sergeant, E-5   1962-1966

- Completed two years of training in Management, Import/Export Operations and Marketing
- Involved in developing a slide presentation for training purposes
- Produced relief maps for military use
- In charge of security files at Command Staff College, Virginia
- Top Secret Clearance
- Captain's Aide: U.S.S. Galveston
- Selected as Marine of the Month
- Honorable Discharge

DOUGLAS J. KLATT

COMBINATION

502 Cove Drive
Prospect Heights, IL 60070

708/555-8229

OBJECTIVE:	**Retail Management**
	A position where profit-building skills would be utilized.
EXPERIENCE:	■ More than nine years in retail management -- including four years in multi-unit supervision -- with full profit / loss responsibilities.
	■ Handle computerized bookkeeping, loss prevention, inventory control and financial statement preparation.
	■ Experience in creative product merchandising and promotions planning.
	■ Effectively hire, train and supervise store personnel in professional customer service and sales.
EMPLOYMENT:	Dad's Video, Arlington Heights, IL 12/81-Present
	District Manager
	In charge of all procedures and operations at three video stores, in a chain of 32.
	Manage up to 25 employees in customer relations, store decorating and the design of creative window displays.
	Plan and implement special in-store promotions and merchandising strategies.
	Determine store layouts and best uses of P.O.P displays.
	Responsible for general ledger and journal updating, as well as accounting activities at all three stores.
	Utilize a menu-driven computer system.
	Work directly with suppliers and contractors on a daily basis.
	Maintain high worker morale and dedication.
	* Currently manage this chain's #1 store.
EDUCATION:	North Central Michigan College, Petoskey, MI 1980-1981
	* Overall GPA: 3.8/4.0
	Successful completion of classes in:
	-- Management -- Accounting
	-- Business Law -- Economics
	Escanaba High School, Escanaba, MI
	Graduate 1980

EDWARD P. REESE   COMBINATION

308 East Thurston Drive
Palatine, IL 60067   708/555-1756

OBJECTIVE: A position utilizing an extensive background in Management, Sales and Operations.

EXPERIENCE:
- More than seven years in sales and management, including full profit/loss responsibility for major territories.

- Experience in market research, strategic planning and competitive analysis; assist in product introduction and promotion.

- Assist in general public relations and the acquisition of new accounts; communicate with key clientele in a professional manner.

- Sales staff hiring, supervision and performance tracking; design and implement specialized training and sales incentive programs.

- Budget development and sales forecasting; experience in full department management, procedure development and the streamlining of operations.

EMPLOYMENT: Frito-Lay, Inc., Chicago, IL   5/83-Present
District Manager   1/86-Present
Effectively manage a staff of 57 in sales, office support, warehousing activities and employee supervision.
Create and assign sales territories.
Train sales representatives and conduct monthly market reviews.
Responsible for inventory control and timely product procurement.
Develop sales incentives programs; plan and conduct sales presentations; entertain key buyers and managers.
Monitor budgets and monitor maintenance schedules for 50 vehicles.
Control all fleet activity for the Chicago branch, including the financial and geographic review of route additions.

-- Planned/implemented sales training programs; reduced turnover by 20 percent.
-- Chicago area sales have expanded $2 million per year in the last four years.
-- Sales for 1991 are projected at $13 million.

Sales and Operations Manager   9/84-1/86
Duties included sales staff training and the generation of computer reports for sales monitoring and product ordering.
Developed office procedures and maintained accurate inventories.
Handled financial and geographic updates and additions to routes.

Territory Manager   1/84-9/84
Responsible for pre-selling product for two route sales representatives, including the setup of secondary displays.
Negotiated directly with store managers for increased shelf space.

Route Sales Representative 5/83-1/84

Managed more than 200 accounts and the sale, delivery and merchandising of product lines to major chains and independent retailers.
Involved in full route updating and expansion.

Presser Tuckpointing and Glass Block Windows, Inc., Chicago, IL 1977-1983

Effectively owned and operated a professional masonry firm.
Trained and supervised nine employees in construction, service and office activities.

American Turners, N.W., Chicago, IL 1976-1983
Athletic Director

Responsible for a physical education program for 850 members of this unique social and physical development club.
Determined monthly tuition rates and salaries of coaches.
Public relations duties included the coordination of shows, exhibitions, fund raisers and various public events.

-- Coached a team of traveling gymnasts which ranked second place in statewide competition, 1983; ranked third place in 1982.

EDUCATION:

Triton College, River Grove, IL
Completed a course in Business Management

Anheuser-Busch, Inc., St. Louis, MO
Attended nine bi-annual weekend seminars on sales and operations over four years.

Carl Schurz High School, Chicago, IL
Graduate

HOWIE R. SAMPSON   *COMBINATION*

134 Lake Blvd. #619
Buffalo Grove, IL 60089   708/555-5915

OBJECTIVE: Sales / Marketing Management / Administration

EXPERIENCE:
- Comprehensive sales, marketing and management experience, including full profit/loss responsibilities in major markets.

- Manage both staff and line departments, with proven abilities in accounting, financial management, labor relations, contract negotiation and general administration.

- Sales staff hiring, supervision and motivation; plan and implement training programs with solid written and oral communications skills.

- Market research, long/short term strategic planning and competitive analysis; handle sales forecasting, budget management and cost control; establish dealer goals and objectives.

EMPLOYMENT: Soccer Laboratories, Glenview, IL   1/90-Present
Sales Representative
Responsible for inside sales of pharmaceuticals to hospitals, nursing homes, and pharmacies for this major producer of generic products.
* Developed a strong account base through cold calling and increased sales to dormant accounts; recognized for an excellent record of progress and sales growth.
* Reactivated a major, high-volume account and increased sales 12 percent.
* Accepted two promotions to larger, more profitable territories, which continue to expand.

Saab-Scania of America, Inc. Elk Grove, IL   1980-1989
Regional Manager - Central Region
Managed all automobile marketing functions for 22 central states.
Supervised 34 field personnel, as well as 15 employees in warehousing and office support; restored worker morale and dealer credibility.
Created and implemented a restructuring program and increased dealer body from 84 to 125.
* Increased sales fourfold to $250 million in car sales and $24 million in parts sales.
* Responsible for turnaround of this region to profitability in 15 months.

Minnesota Tractor Co., a unit of Fiat-Allis Inc., Bloomington, MN   1978-1980
General Manager
Responsible for P&L and all operations of this unit, including policy development, procedure streamlining and the development of improved methods related to sales planning, reporting and inventory control.

* Created and implemented a successful advertising and public relations program.
* Managed short & long term strategic planning and budgeting systems.
* Instrumental in converting from a manual to a computerized system.
* Interfaced with corporate headquarters; completed special assignments.
* Credited with restoring profitability of this unit in the first ten months.

Volvo of America Corp., Torrence, CA   1975-1978
Administrative Manager / Controller, Des Plaines, IL
Responsible for finance, real estate, personnel, accounting and legal activities for the Midwest Division, with 85 dealers in eight states.
Involved in negotiations with banks, as well as in the streamlining of data processing and office/information systems.
Handled budget preparation & control; involved in cost-effective purchasing.
* Assumed additional responsibilities in dealer development and business management.
* Acted as Administrative Assistant to Division President in marketing and numerous special projects.
* Accepted the following duties during last year at this position:

Dealer Development Manager / Controller
Appointed dealers and developed/implemented policies and procedures for 26 states.
Established, organized and implemented all business management, marketing, dealer plans and objectives for the region.
Worked directly with corporate headquarters in forming and creating operating standards for dealers.
* Analyzed and improved training requirements, both internally and within the dealer organization.

PRIOR EXPERIENCE:

Gene Wulbert Ford, Inc., Oak Park, IL		1973-1975
Secretary-Treasurer and Business Manager		
U.S. Life Mutual Funds Management, New York, NY		1973
Regional Manager		
Harris Chernin, Inc., Chicago, IL		1970-1972
Controller		
Howe, Barnes & Johnson, Inc.,		1968-1970
Registered Representative		
Carol Buick, Inc. and related companies, Evanston, IL		1960-1968
Controller		
Walton Motors, Inc., Chicago, IL		1956-1960
Staff Accountant		

EDUCATION:

I.B.M. Executive Concepts Course, San Jose, CA   1976
Completed training at I.B.M. Center

                                                                    1950-1952
DePaul University, Chicago, IL   1952-1954
B.S.C.

WALLACE GEORGE   COMBINATION

30 Johnson Drive #1715
Buffalo Grove, IL 60089   708/555-9737

OBJECTIVE: Project Manager
                    A position utilizing experience with computerized telecommunication systems.

SUMMARY: - Proven ability to establish and maintain a personal rapport and relate well to co-workers at all levels of experience; solid written and oral communication skills.

                    - Prioritize tasks, handle multiple projects simultaneously and consistently meet deadlines and budget constraints.

                    - Through personalized management skills, effectively train, motivate and evaluate support staff in technical product lines and client relations.

EXPERIENCE: Telemanagement & Equipment Corporation (TEC), Northbrook, IL   1989-Present
                    Project Manager
                    Supervise the installation of telephone systems at hotels and motels, including site surveying, the preparation/analysis of bid specifications and contract approval.
                    Provide full customer training and support on a group and individual basis.

                    Crosscom National, Inc., Northbrook, IL   1988-1989
                    Account Manager
                    Responsible for major accounts including multi-million dollar Toys 'R Us.
                    Coordinated installation and service activities for telephone systems used by national retail chains.

                    Northern Telecom, Inc., Arlington Heights, IL   1986-1988
                    Field Installer
                    Handled installation and quality control testing of DMS 100/200 digital switching equipment for Illinois Bell and other phone companies.
                    Trained new employees and maintained excellent customer relations.
                    - Earned commendation for "Outstanding Work Performed During a Difficult Installation."
                    - Selected to complete in-house training courses.

                    Teradyne, Inc., Deerfield, IL   1984-1986
                    Final Processor / Stager; promoted to **Installation Technician.**
                    Installed 4TEL test systems interfaced with analog and digital telephone switches, including Automatic Electric and Northern Telecom systems.
                    Duties included new employee training and orientation.
                    - Received numerous Certificates of Accomplishment for completing in-house training courses.

EDUCATION: Parkland College, Champaign, IL
                    A.A. Degree: Business Administration   1982

ELIZABETH HIZER   *COMBINATION*

1376 Wyndham Circle
Palatine, IL 60067   708/555-0116

OBJECTIVE: Customer Service / Reception
                   A challenging position where professional skills will be utilized.

EXPERIENCE: - More than ten years of combined experience in sales and customer service, including account acquisition and management.

                   - Determine and meet specific customer needs in a professional manner.

                   - Handle account updating and spreadsheets with Lotus 1-2-3; familiar with general ledgers and bookkeeping.

EMPLOYMENT: **Co-Owner/Operator**   9/89-1/91
                   U-Wash, Me-Dry Casselberry, FL
                   Responsible for sales promotions and advertising for this busy laundromat.
                   Trained and supervised four employees.
                   Planned and implemented operating budgets and reviewed P&L statements; utilized Lotus to manage accounting information.

                   Office Manager   6/81-10/88
                   Glencoe News Agency, Glencoe, IL
                   In charge of customer service for a newspaper distributor with over 3,000 individual home delivery outlets and 15 retail newspaper outlets. Handled customer questions and problems regarding the sale of newspapers including the *Wall Street Journal, New York Times,* and *Chicago Tribune.*

                   *   Worked directly with publishers, regional distributors and customers.
                   *   Responsible for cost-effective dispatch, billing, expediting and purchasing of items required for distribution.
                   *   Supervised ten employees, interfaced with vendors and managed all aspects of accounts payable/receivable.

                   Commercial Teller   9/80-6/81
                   The Winnetka Bank, Winnetka, IL
                   Maintained accurate cash balances and handled numerous monetary transactions with clients.

                   Office Assistant   6/76-9/80
                   AMBCO Capital Corporation, Northbrook, IL
                   Maintained positive customer relations at this finance company specializing in high-risk automobile insurance.

EDUCATION: Bemidji State University, Bemidji, MN   1978-1980
                   Completion of courses in Communications and Psychology.

BRUCE J. BARRET *COMBINATION*

351 Mohawk Lane
Glenview, IL 60025   708/555-2705

EXPERIENCE:	• More than 12 years of fixed income sales experience with a major firm, covering commercial banks, money managers and public pension funds.
	• Extensive relationships within the Ohio and Western Pennsylvania banking communities.
	• Comprehensive knowledge of products which include OTC options and swap related activities.

EMPLOYMENT:

Universal Partners, Inc., Chicago, IL
Vice President, Marketing   8/90-Present
Responsible for marketing money management services -- for a registered investment advisor -- to pension consultants, pension plan sponsors, corporations and high net worth individuals.

Rogers, Peabody & Company, Inc., Chicago, IL   4/78-8/90
Vice President, Fixed Income Sales   8/86-8/90
Covered a variety of institutional clients including major commercial banks, thrifts, public pension funds, money managers and state governments.
Geographic concentration of important relationships in Ohio and Western Pennsylvania.
Products included U.S. Governments, agencies, mortgages, CMO's, asset-backs, corporates, OTC options, swaps and futures.
Business included relative value sector swaps, yield curve arbitrage, option-related strategies and matched-funding transactions.
Transferred to Chicago regional office as part of a company reorganization.

Vice President, Fixed Income Sales, Cleveland, OH   4/78-8/86
Marketed taxable, fixed income products to commercial banks, thrifts, insurance companies and state & local governments.
Directly supervised operations of a six-person institutional sales branch from 6/84-8/86.
Hired and trained staff; managed all aspects of sales and client servicing.
- Achieved shareholder status in 1982.
- Promoted from Vice President in 1980.

Equibank, N.A., Pittsburgh, PA   6/76-4/78
Vice President, Manager: Taxable Trading Desk
Supervised operation of a seven-person trading desk, including hiring and training.
Coordinated training with the sales manager for optimum staff performance.

EDUCATION:

Kent State University, Kent, OH
M.B.A., Finance, 1973
B.B.A., Finance, 1970

JAMES C. COTS *COMBINATION*

14 West Oakdale #2A 312/555-8100 Ofc.
Chicago, IL 60657 312/555-4014 Res.

EXPERIENCE:
- More than five years in retail leasing and commercial sales, including full responsibility for market research, competitive analysis and account acquisition/management.

- Handle strategic planning and sales forecasting; familiar with Lotus 1-2-3 and WordPerfect as well as NPV and IRR calculations.

- Developed/co-developed 49,000 s.f. of retail and office space valued in excess of $6 million since 1988.

- Completed all courses towards CCIM Designation.

EMPLOYMENT:

Johnson Realty Group, Chicago, IL 1987-Present
Account Manager
Responsible for retail leasing and commercial property sales.
Act as leasing agent for retail property owners.
Proven ability to develop profitable relationships with major clientele.

- Completed 30 deals ranging from 1,000 to 15,000 s.f. in 1990.
- Cumulative dollar volume of deals in excess of $10 million, 1989-present.
- Sales of commercial and retail properties have exceeded $3 million per year since 1987.

Plotkin & Company, Chicago, IL 1985-1987
Broker
Directly involved in the opening of this company.
Worked extensively with national retailers including K-Mart.

Acted as lead broker for:
- Riverplace shopping center, 80,000 s.f., in Lansing, IL.
- Plaza Del Prado shopping center, 125,000 s.f., Glenview, IL.
- Oak Creek Plaza shopping center, 360,000 s.f., Mundelein, IL.

Wasilov & Zifkin Distributors, Philadelphia, PA 1980-1985
President / Owner
Successfully imported, distributed and serviced high-end restaurant equipment.

- Sales grew from $30,000 to $400,000 in first four years.
- This business was sold in 1985 at a substantial profit.

EDUCATION:

Michigan State University, East Lansing, MI
B.A. Degree, Geography 1975

University of Michigan, Ann Arbor, MI
Teaching Certificate 1976

6
COVER LETTERS

When you know the name of the company and person to whom you will be sending your resume, then a cover letter is essential. Here you can state more specifically what type of work you're applying for, which is especially valuable if you omitted an OBJECTIVE on your resume. It also gives you the chance to write less formally about who you are, what you can accomplish in the position, and what you know about the firm. This last item can really help separate you from the crowd. You must research the firm whenever possible and demonstrate that you know:

1. What types of products and/or services they produce.
2. Their major markets: business, general consumer, national or international.
3. What their current hiring needs are and how you can help fill those needs.

General Tips

1. Always send a cover letter with your resume and personalize it by researching the company. Exceptions can be made for blind box ads, but if it looks like an exceptional position, then by all means include a letter addressed to "Ladies/Gentlemen:", "Dear Hiring Authority:", or "Dear Prospective Employer:". Use a colon (:) when you've never spoken to the individual and a comma when you have.

   See page 206 for resource materials available from your local library.

2. Address your letters to an individual whenever possible. If you don't have a name, call the company and get the exact spelling of the hiring authority's name and their job title. If that's not available, send it to the personnel manager, human resources representative or corporate recruiter, with their name if possible.

3. Make your letters brief and to the point, and they stand a much better chance of getting read. Some employers skip the letter entirely and get to it only after they like what they see in your resume, so keep your letter down to three or four short paragraphs to increase its readability.
4. Letters should always be typed. Try to match paper colors of resumes and letters, but don't worry too much about this. White goes well with everything, is easy to correct on your typewriter and doesn't look mass produced. It also looks more personal and immediate.
5. Proofread your letter as closely as your resume. Proofread once for content, then once for grammar and typing mistakes. Then read it backwards, and have someone else read it too.

Writing The Cover Letter

Expanding on the points mentioned earlier, your cover letter should contain:

1. The exact title of the position you are seeking. If that's not possible, then the general type of work for which you are applying.
2. Why you want to work for the company. Remember: "What Can You Do For Me?"
3. A dazzling sample of what you know about the company: product lines, marketing strategies, their quality and quantity of clientele and where they stand among their competitors:

"I understand you will be introducing your new dishwasher in the Yugoslavian market this Fall. I have several ideas that may help you compete with Maytag's established line."

Obviously, not everyone wants to be a product manager, but you get the picture: check annual reports at the library, also newspaper and magazine articles, trade journals, even *The Nightly Business Report* on public television. Any and all sources can prove valuable in your research.

4. Whether you are willing to travel or relocate, if this is a factor related to the line of work, such as outside sales or consulting. You may omit this if it is not requested, or if you <u>are not</u> willing to travel or relocate.

5. Other specifics about yourself or the job. If the posting says: "Include salary requirements", and not salary history, give them a desired salary range and avoid a specific number. For example: "upper $40s/year, negotiable". You may include this in a letter, but if they ask for salary requirements <u>and</u> salary history, include them on a separate salary history sheet, and end the page with "Salary requirements are open to negotiation". See the Salary History example on page 199.

- TIPSTER -
When mailing your resume and cover letter, be sure to use large 9"x12" catalog envelopes. This keeps your resume flat and presentable, avoiding the "accordion" look of folded resumes. Folding can actually crack the type off of certain papers. Yes, this costs more to mail, about 52 cents, but it's worth it. Next to a stack of #10 envelopes, yours stands out even before it's opened and is much easier to read. This is especially recommended for executives with 2-3 page presentations.

The cover letter must generate interest in you and the resume which follows. You then close with requesting an interview or telling the reader when you will be contacting them to arrange an interview. Personal contact shows you're aggressive and interested in their firm specifically.

Call the firm on the date you mail your cover letter and resume and try to speak directly with the manager or hiring authority. If that's impossible, at least talk to the personnel representative. Tell him your name and that you've sent a resume in application for the position. Try to strike-up a conversation about your qualifications and how they're just right for the job. But don't oversell yourself if the person sounds too busy to talk. Of course, if the advertisement or posting says NO CALLS PLEASE, then don't call--unless you can anonymously learn the hiring authority's name and/or title from the receptionist. In that case, try calling that person directly and inquire about opportunities in your field, as if you've never seen the ad and heard about them or their company through industry contacts or a friend. Be prepared to handle yourself well if you try this!

Keep a detailed list or card file of resumes sent to whom and on what date. You should call the company three to four days after sending your resume and try to speak with the actual hiring authority. Tell them you want to confirm they've received your resume and that you would like to arrange an interview. Try to speak directly with the manager or supervisor, but if that's impossible, try the personnel representative. Be sure not to make a pest of yourself! Hounding anyone on the telephone is perceived as pushy and desperate.

As a personnel representative, I came across an extreme example of this problem with an applicant whom the manager and I had already interviewed. We agreed that although the candidate had energy and some degree of experience, it just wasn't the kind of experience we thought was essential to the job. After learning he had not been hired, the applicant called our office at least ten times over the next two weeks to tell us more about his background and why he thought we had a great company. He drove the receptionist crazy and only confirmed our suspicions of immaturity.

If the manager or representative refuses to speak with you or set an interview, give it one more try the next day or two. Then sit tight or send a follow-up letter like the example on page 197. Don't be discouraged by the standard "we're reviewing the applications and will be arranging interviews as soon as we've screened them all." This is the standard "don't call us, we'll call you." And it's not without justification. Sometimes employers really *do* want to sift through the resumes first and then decide who to meet.

The whole idea of resume follow-up is to drop your name into the mind of the manager or representative and distance yourself from the silent stack of resumes. If you can set an interview, fine. But remember that employers have time constraints and perhaps hundreds of resumes to screen, so don't be dismayed.

Some people approach their job search with a "me against them" attitude: "them" being the prospective employer. They see only a wall of indifference from hiring managers and personnel representatives. This can be fatal to a job search, and as hard as it may seem, you need to project yourself as an ally to all staff and managers at the target company.

7

EXAMPLES:

COVER LETTERS AND

FOLLOW-UP LETTERS

REFERENCE AND

SALARY HISTORY SHEETS

JEFFERY H. CROCKETT
57 Weidner Road
Buffalo Grove, IL 60089
708/555-3086

JOB-SPECIFIC LETTER

Mr. Robert Anderson
Anderson Marketing, Inc.
835 Lincolnwood Drive,
Chicago, IL 60690

Dear Mr. Anderson:

Given the excellent reputation of your firm, (or Anderson Marketing/company name) I am submitting my resume in application for an Account Management position. Specifically, I am seeking to better utilize my profit-building skills in account prospecting, acquisition and management.

In my position with Arty Incentives, I have proven my ability to create highly profitable, personalized relationships with key clientele at hundreds of companies. I've executed complex sales with a strong knowledge of product lines, (you could list several here) industry trends and of course, the customer's specific needs.

My success thus far is a result of comprehensive research and taking an interactive role in a client's business. This allows me to design and implement customized incentive programs while always keeping a sharp eye on bottom-line results.

I am willing to travel (and/or relocate) for the right opportunity, and can provide excellent references at your request. Please let me know as soon as possible when we may meet for a personal interview. (or: I will be contacting you soon to arrange a personal interview) Thank you for your time and consideration.

Sincerely,

Jeffrey H. Crockett

enc.

THOMAS F. DEACON

GENERAL BOILERPLATE LETTER

**319 Verde Drive
Arlington Heights, IL 60004
(708) 555-5134**

Dear Hiring Executive (or Manager):

I am exploring the possibility of joining your staff, and have enclosed my resume for your review. Specifically, I am seeking to better utilize my talents in (staff training, general accounting, production operations and/or sales, etc...).

My background includes full responsibility for (account prospecting, sales presentations and effective client relations). I've developed excellent contacts at hundreds of large and small businesses, and I feel that this can be extremely valuable to your firm.

Throughout my career, I've proven my ability to work effectively with management and staff at all levels of experience. Most importantly, I have demonstrated my ability to determine and meet the needs of the customer in a professional, yet personalized manner.

I am available for an interview at your convenience to discuss how my education and experience could benefit your company. Please contact me at the above number or address in order to arrange a meeting. I am looking forward to meeting you and discussing the possibility of joining your company.

Thank you for your time and consideration.

Sincerely,

Thomas F. Deacon

enc.

Alice Shaminski
1145 Marlboro Lane
Rolling Knolls, IL 69896
708/555-8976

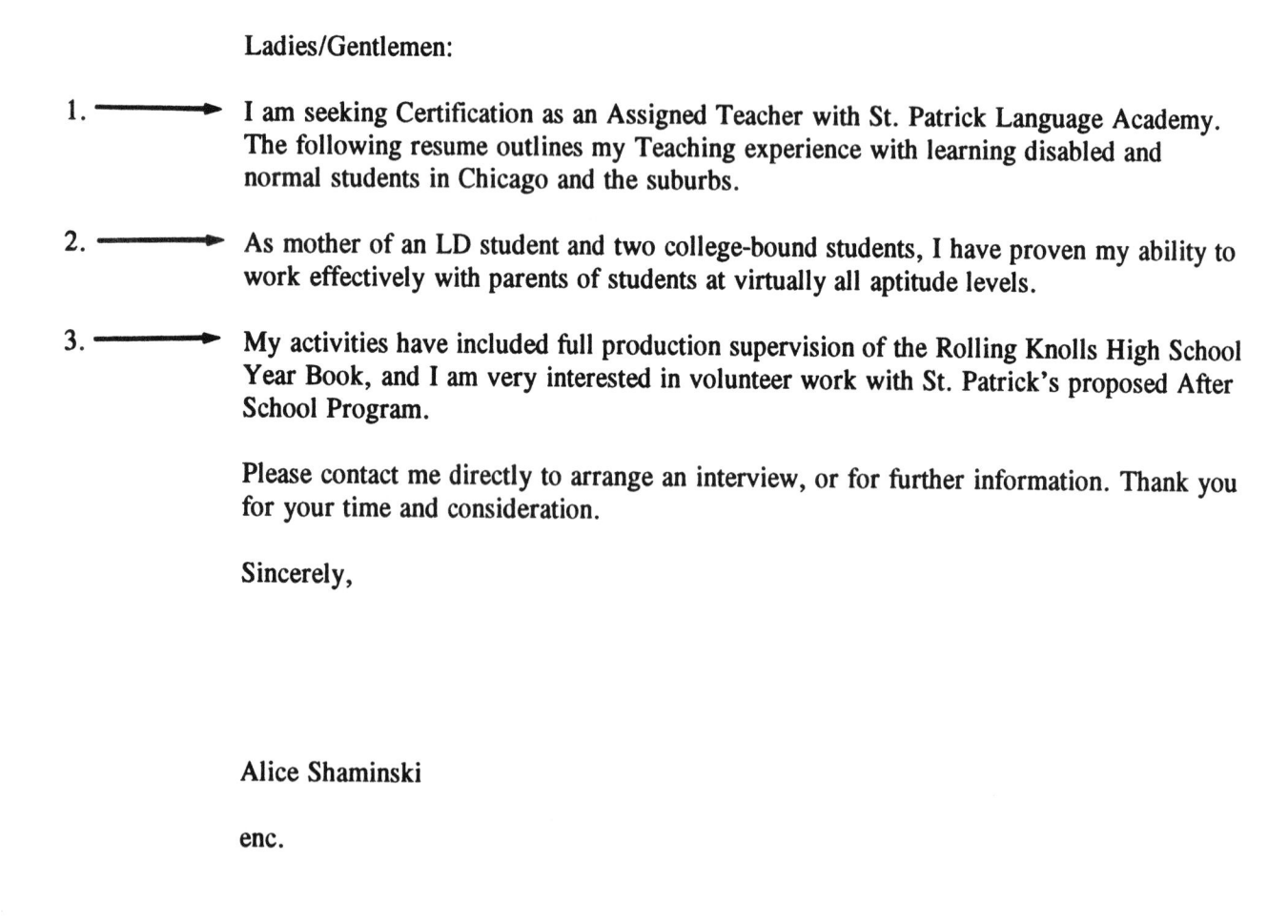

COVER LETTER

Ladies/Gentlemen:

1. ⟶ I am seeking Certification as an Assigned Teacher with St. Patrick Language Academy. The following resume outlines my Teaching experience with learning disabled and normal students in Chicago and the suburbs.

2. ⟶ As mother of an LD student and two college-bound students, I have proven my ability to work effectively with parents of students at virtually all aptitude levels.

3. ⟶ My activities have included full production supervision of the Rolling Knolls High School Year Book, and I am very interested in volunteer work with St. Patrick's proposed After School Program.

Please contact me directly to arrange an interview, or for further information. Thank you for your time and consideration.

Sincerely,

Alice Shaminski

enc.

NOTES: (1) Alice was presenting her qualifications directly to a committee for full-time status where she was currently a substitute. She was applying in Chicago where she had minimal work experience, so I placed Chicago before suburbs. (2) LD is o.k. after spelling out learning disabled in the first paragraph. Mentioning her children shows she has actual experience raising an LD child. (3) Demonstrates a strong interest in extra-curricular activities and a background in St. Patrick's proposed program.

Lucy Dish
9876 College Avenue #213
DeKalb, IL 60115
815/555-2474

BOILER PLATE COVER LETTER
BLIND AD / ENTRY LEVEL

Dear Prospective Employer: *(or Dear Hiring Manager:)*

In the interest of exploring employment opportunities with your organization, I've enclosed my resume for your review. Specifically, I am seeking to expand my experience (and training) in (office management, accounting, data processing, etc.).

My strong work ethic and attention to detail would prove extremely valuable to a company which makes customer service its top priority. I am self-motivated and energetic, and communicate well with customers, staff and management to get the job done.

Please let me know as soon as possible when we may meet to discuss mutual interests. Thank you for your time, and I look forward to your response.

Sincerely,

Lucy Dish

enc.

Alfred E. Plate
574 West Rita Drive
Chicago, IL 60692
312/555-9276

*PROFESSIONAL / EXECUTIVE
BOILER PLATE COVER LETTER*

(**Note:** If name or title is not available,
you may use Ladies/Gentlemen, Dear Hiring
Manager or Dear Prospective Employer)

Mr. Edward Smith
Director of Product Development,
Necco Corporation
598 LaSalle Street, Suite 213
Chicago, IL 60606

Dear Mr. Smith:

The position of (position name) advertised in last Sunday's (newspaper name) seems tailor-made for me. My experience with (last or current employer) involved responsibility for (several duties listed in the ad), and my efforts resulted in a 20 percent reduction in overhead for 1989. The enclosed resume outlines my qualifications and accomplishments.

I now seek to better utilize my (supervisory/design/organizational, etc.) skills with an industry leader such as (company name, if applicable). I am willing to travel or relocate and my salary requirements are negotiable. (You may omit 'negotiable' and give a range, such as 'upper $40s per year' if requested in the ad.)

I will contact you during the first week of August (or *soon*) to arrange an interview. Meanwhile, please feel free to give me a call should you require any further information on my background.

Sincerely,

Alfred E. Plate

enc.

Debra Roberts 897 Salem Trail #B2 Northbrook, IL 60062 707/555-1265

FOLLOW-UP LETTER

(**Note:** Call or send a note like this the day after your interview to re-state your interest in the position and thank your interviewer.)

Jane Alvin
Regional Sales Manager,
Compaq Corporation
398 Microchip Drive
Chicago, IL 60683

Dear Ms. Alvin,

Thank you for your time and an excellent (or very informative) interview on (Monday). It was a pleasure meeting you and I was most impressed by the high professional standards demonstrated by your staff.

I am certain my (Sales, Marketing or Management) skills would prove extremely valuable as a member of your Northwestern Regional Sales Team. Your product line is excellent, and your company has proven its ability to reach both new and expanding markets.

Once again, thank you for your consideration and I look forward to new career challenges with your excellent firm.

Sincerely,

Debra Roberts

REFERENCE SHEET EXAMPLE

JOHN H. DOAN, JR.

REFERENCES

Business:

Bruce Gin, President
Fairfield Marine, Inc.
5739 Dixie Highway
Fairfield, OH 45014
513/555-0825

Brian Krixen, Partner
Ernst & Young
150 South Wacker Drive
Chicago, IL 60606
312/555-1800

Charlie Kinnock, VP Sales/Marketing
Jayco Inc.
P.O. Box 460
Middlebury, IN 46540
219/555-5861

Jim E. Shields, President
Shields Southwest Sales, Inc.
1008 Brady Avenue N.W.
Atlanta, GA 30318
404/555-1133

Personal:

Richard Baeson, Yamaha
Business Development Manager
P.O. Box 8234
Barrington, IL 60011
708/555-4446

Bob Redson, Salesman
Central Photo Engraving
712 South Prairie Avenue
Chicago, IL 60616
708/555-9119

Dan Linder, CPA
Conklin Accounting & Tax Service
5262 South Rt. 83 #308
Willowbrook, IL 60514
708/555-8800

Baden Powell, Manager
Banker's Leasing Association
3201 Lake Cook Road
Northbrook, IL 60062
708/555-5353

STEVEN A. ROGERS

SALARY HISTORY EXAMPLE

Salary History

(Annual Basis)

People Search, Inc.
Human Resources Representative — $30,000

Anderson Employment, Inc.
Staff Writer — Up to $25,000: Commission Based

National Van Lines
Corporate Recruiter — $24,000

Nuclear News
Assistant Editor — $23,000

Professional Career Consultants
Writer and Branch Manager — Up to $29,000: Commission Based

Notes:

* You could also add: Current salary requirements are open to negotiation.

If salary *requirements* are requested, you could also add:

* Currently seeking a position in the low $30s per year.

Remember that this could label you as over- or under-priced for the position. That's one reason they ask for it in the first place.

Also remember that unless you feel it's essential, include salary history and/or requirements only when requested by the employer.

8

BROADCAST LETTERS

Some people swear by them, others swear at them. They're called Broadcast or Personal Sales Letters, and in some cases, they can effectively replace a resume and help you get an interview. The Broadcast letter relieves the hiring authority from the "just another resume" mentality, and offers a viable alternative. Here you emphasize knowledge and experience directly applicable to the position at hand.

Broadcast letters are best used when no position has been advertised, and you're looking to spark interest in your qualifications with an executive, manager, or whomever is the hiring authority. I recommend them only to those seeking executive-level or managerial positions which may or may not already exist at a particular organization. They must be sent directly to the person who would appreciate and possibly hire someone with your qualifications.

General Format

Begin the text of your letter with the most impressive, unique aspects of your career. You have to immediately grasp the attention of this busy executive and entice him or her take a minute to get to know you. After all, they haven't requested any resumes or applications, why should they read yours?

Start with a brief summary of where you are now and what you have accomplished with your current or most recent employer. In these attention-getting paragraphs, capitalize your position title(s):

- As chief design engineer with Compu-Best, I managed a staff of six and was solely responsible for acquiring this firm's largest overseas account.

OR:

- As Senior Financial Officer for a big-eight accounting firm, my efforts have streamlined collection procedures and reduced delinquent accounts by 12 percent.

- As Director of Marketing for General Motor's appliance division, I planned and implemented marketing strategies which increased refrigerator sales 21 percent in FY 1989.

Notice in the example above that you don't detail exactly how you accomplished the sales increase, the reader will have to call you in to find out. Also, using FY rather than Fiscal Year shows a certain respect to both your own and the reader's experience in senior-level management.

- I speak five languages fluently, have traveled extensively and acquired profitable accounts throughout Europe and Japan. Throughout my career, I've been instrumental in long and short-term budget planning resulting in the successful penetration of markets previously considered inaccessible.

What languages, what specific markets, in what countries? Don't tell them in this letter. Here's where you generate curiosity and make them want to meet such an achiever. Just don't let your wording sound cocky or you may be perceived as a snob.

In the introductory paragraph, you don't need to list your current employer, which ensures confidentiality. Although this is an advantage over all but certain functional resumes, remember that you still must include your name, and if your industry is small and close-knit, your current employer may hear that you're looking for a new position. However, this is unlikely and most employers will respect your privacy.

In the final paragraph, tell the reader when you will be available for an interview and request that they contact you as soon as possible to arrange a meeting. Whenever possible however, you should take the initiative and call the employer to set an interview:

I will be calling you within one week to arrange a personal interview. Meanwhile, please feel free to contact me for any further information you may require.

OR:

I will be in Boston September 5th through the 10th and can be reached at the Sheraton Hotel downtown, 212/555-8847. I look forward to discussing mutual interests with you.

Sincerely,

Ronald E. Jones

MICHAEL T. SMITH
576 Cherry Street
Broadview, IL 60789
609/555-1736

BROADCAST LETTER

Mr. James Williamson, President
Armstrong Associates
518 College Avenue
DeKalb, IL 60115

Dear Mr. Williamson:

As Director of Life Insurance Sales for a Fortune 500 firm, I have proven my ability to direct a sales force of 1,250 while creating and implementing innovative marketing strategies. One such strategy resulted in a 14 percent sales increase in the first quarter of FY 1988.

In view of the phenomenal growth your firm has experienced in group health sales, I would like to present a synopsis of my qualifications in application for a position in Life Insurance Marketing with Armstrong Associates. Throughout my career I have:

- Created marketing concepts which increased sales in low-income territories by 12 percent in the third quarter of FY 1989.

- Designed and authored a comprehensive sales training manual, detailing product benefits and in-home sales strategies for clients at various income levels.

- Reduced sales staff turnover by 5 percent in FY 1989 through more effective interface with key personnel and recruitment staff.

- Updated descriptions of sales positions and increased worker output while decreasing base salaries.

I earned my MBA from The University of Chicago and continue to conduct a night course in Marketing at this institution.

I would appreciate the opportunity to meet with you personally to discuss how my experience may benefit Armstrong Associates. Please contact me at your earliest convenience to arrange an interview. I can be reached at the above phone number after 7:00 p.m. weekdays. Thank you for your time and consideration.

Sincerely,

Michael T. Smith

9

USING YOUR RESUME EFFECTIVELY

The writing is finished, you've had it copied, typeset, or laser printed, and it looks absolutely impeccable. It also reads like a charm, does not over- or under-sell your qualifications, and uses direct, high-impact, easy to understand language. Now what do you do with it?

Before you do anything, RESEARCH, RESEARCH, RESEARCH. Whenever possible, review annual reports, articles and summaries of companies in resource books at your local library, many of which are listed on pages 206-208. This cannot be over emphasized, because applicants who show a real knowledge of a company stand a much better chance of being hired by that company. Use key facts about a company's market, product lines and current condition in your cover letter. Even if this amounts to one or two lines, it helps differentiate you from the pack of applicants who send resumes to every company on earth. Of course, research isn't possible with blind ads. But if you have the time, write a letter emphasizing items in the advertisement.

Resumes are most commonly used to respond to advertisements, but they have many other uses:

1. **Networking.** This is the best - if least common - use of your resume. Make sure everyone you know in the industry has a copy of your resume if you are out of work. If you are still employed, be sure to maintain confidentiality and offer your resume only to people you really trust. Give copies to your family and friends, or anyone at all you think might know a company president, manager, supervisor or influential professional in your field. Acquaintances from professional groups and associations can be extremely valuable.

2. **Employment Agencies and Headhunters.** Don't underestimate the power of an employment agency or placement professional. They often have positions which are not advertised due to the client firm's desire for confidentiality or detachment from the screening process. Register with the more established firms and avoid the sleazy operations that make promises they can't keep. Avoid paying resume writing and clerical charges disguised as "out of pocket expenses". Unless you really believe the agency can help you out, let the employer pay the fees. In general, never pay for a job.

3. **Cold Calling.** Drop in off the street, in business attire of course, and fill out applications at businesses in your area. Try to research these companies first, and leave a resume with your application. Call the hiring authority the next day to follow-up.

4. **Different Types of Advertisements.** Blind box ads are used by companies that don't want to be identified, and they pay extra for the privilege. This keeps their own employees from learning about the position and confidentiality is maintained. This type of ad also relieves the firm of maintaining their public image by sending the ubiquitous rejection letter. Respond to blind ads if the position seems right for you, but don't expect much. You can't call or research the company, you don't know where it's located, and you can't personalize a cover letter. Don't forget advertisements in trade journals and magazines related to your field. By the way, the firm placing the blind ad could be your own!

5. **College Placement Offices.** Send a few copies of your resume to the placement office at your old school. Even if you haven't seen the place in years, you never know what this may lead to.

6. **Career/Job Fairs.** These are great places to drop-off resumes with many companies and save time, travel, and postage. Of course, a cover letter is not expected and these fairs offer the chance to have mini interviews right on the spot. There are free job fairs at colleges and hotels listed in many Sunday newspapers. Begin with the fairs that charge no admission fees and review the list of firms before you attend.

RESOURCE MATERIALS

Listings, catalogs and great books

Many of the books listed below cross-reference companies by industry and provide insight on company size and products, as well as names of human resource personnel and key managers. I highly recommend *Rites of Passage at $100,000+* by John Lucht. Even if you're no where near the $100,000 job range, this book is an excellent guide to job changing. It covers the recruitment business and how to make it work for you, personal and non-personal networking, direct mailings, interviewing and much more.

Visit your local library and ask about these books, most of which are listed in *Rites of Passage at $100,000+*, for information on thousands of companies. Also ask about listings and reference materials specific to your industry: advertising, electrical engineering, etc.

America's Corporate Families - Vol. I and *America's Corporate Families and International Affiliates* - Vol. II. By Dun's Marketing Services. Two hard-cover volumes updated annually. Information on more than 11,000 U.S. Parent companies and their 60,000 subsidiaries & divisions.

Commerce Register's Geographical Directories of Manufacturer's. Numerous directories for specific geographical regions. Organized by city, this book provides information on manufacturer's with more than 5 employees in the state or region, including address, telephone, products and sales figures.

Corporate 1000 Yellow Book, International Corporate 1000 Yellow Book and *Over-The-Counter 1000 Yellow Book.* By Monitor Publishing Co. Each lists names, titles, and often direct-dial numbers for key officers, plus outside Board members and their companies.

Directories in Print. By Gale Research, Inc. Published every two years. Companies are organized by industry/discipline. Describes the contents of 10,000 publications including directories, professional and scientific rosters, and other lists and guides.

Directory of Corporate Affiliations. By National Register Publishing Company, Inc. Subtitled *Who Owns Whom.* Lists 40,000 divisions/subsidiaries of over 4,000 U.S. public and private companies. Gives assets, liabilities, net worth, income/earnings and approximate sales. Indexed by geography, (state and city), S.I.C. (Standard Industry Code) and professionals linked with the company, with a cross-reference index of divisions, subsidiaries and affiliates. Also summarizes recent mergers, acquisitions and name changes.

Directory of Executive Recruiters. Lists thousands of executive recruiters; indexed by industry specialties. Includes excellent information on recruitment industry methods.

Dun's Europa. By Dun's Marketing Services. Profiles top 35,000 European manufacturing, distribution, financial and service companies. Listings in both English and indigenous language.

Employment Agencies. By American Business Directories. Lists thousands of employment agencies around the country.

Encyclopedia of Associations. Gale Research, Inc. Four volumes in three books, with detailed information on more than 22,000 U.S. headquartered, non-profit associations and organizations of all kinds.

Encyclopedia of Business Information Sources. Gale Research, Inc. More than 20,000 information sources on 1,280 highly specific subjects ranging from abrasives to zinc. Lists encyclopedias, dictionaries, handbooks, manuals, bibliographies, associations, societies, etc.

Getting Hired In The '90s. By Vicki Spina and Corporate Image Publishers. Published in January, 1993 and available by mail order outside the Chicago area: 1-800-247-6553.

Guide to American Directories. By B. Klein Publications. Updated every two years. Describes content, frequency and cost (if any) of 7,500 directories in a variety of fields (over 300 classifications) with phone numbers.

International Directory of Company Histories. St. James; available from Gale Research, Inc. Volume 2 published in 1990. Gives basic information and histories (1,500-3,000 words each) for about 1,250 companies in the U.S., Canada, U.K. Europe and Japan.

International Directory of Corporate Affiliations. National Register Publishing Company, Inc. Two soft-cover volumes. 1: Non-U.S. holdings of U.S. Parent companies; 2: U.S. and worldwide holdings of foreign enterprises.

Job Hunter's Resource Guide. Gale Research, Inc. Annual, one volume. Lists reference materials for 150 specific professions/occupations. Also has a "how-to" section.

Job Seeker's Guide to Public and Private Companies. Gale Research, Inc. Information on more than 25,000 companies, including corporate overviews, specific job titles and estimated number of openings for each, hiring practices, personnel contacts, employee benefits, application procedures and recruitment activities.

Knock 'Em Dead with Great Answers to Tough Interview Questions. By Martin Yate; Bob Adams Publishers, 238 pages. A great interview primer.

Million Dollar Directory Series. Dun's Marketing Services. A five-volume hard-cover series listing 160,000 public and private U.S. companies. Includes key facts on decision makers, company size and lines of business. This may be hard to find, considering its $1,250 annual lease fee.

Million Dollar Directory of Top 50,000 Companies. Dun's Marketing Services. Covers the top 50,000 companies (net worth) from the *Million Dollar Directory Series.*

Moody's Industrial Manual and News Reports. Moody's Investor's Service. Annual, two volumes. Provides full financial and operating data on every industrial corporation on the NYSE and ASE, plus more than 500 on regional exchanges. Twice-weekly news reports update developments.

Moody's International Manual and New Reports. Moody's Investor Service. Full financial data on over 5,000 international corporations. Twice-weekly news reports update developments.

The National Directory of Addresses and Telephone Numbers. General Information, Inc. Excellent for your mailing list. Provides addresses and phone numbers for U.S. corporations, both alphabetically and by S.I.C. category.

Standard & Poor's Register of Corporations, Directors and Executives. Three volumes with just about everything on major U.S. and Canadian companies and the people who run them.

Standard Directory of Advertisers. National Register Publishing Company, Inc. Lists more than 25,000 U.S. advertiser companies with addresses, phone, sales, number of employees and primary businesses. Also advertising media.

Thomas' Register of American Manufacturers. Thomas Publishing Company. Annual profile of 150,000 manufacturers with their major products and services. Includes 12,000 pages of catalog material and 112,000 registered trade/brand names.

Ward's Business Directory of U.S. Private and Public Companies. Gale Research, Inc. Annual, four volumes. Provides demographic and financial business data on over 85,000 companies. Volumes provide alphabetic and zip-code listings of companies.

Who's Who in America. Marquis Who's Who, Inc. Every two years. Profiles more than 79,000 leaders, decision-makers, and innovators from a variety of fields, including business, governments, journalism, art, diplomacy, law, science, medicine, music and education.

Who's Who in Finance & Industry. Marquis Who's Who, Inc. Gives profiles on more than 22,000 principal decision makers from the fields of banking, insurance, transportation, government regulatory agencies, major corporations, etc.

10

AT LAST: THE INTERVIEW

If you manage to get one interview for every 20 resumes sent to advertisements, you're doing pretty good. Even if you have several interviews booked, don't stop researching, checking advertisements, and sending resumes. Always hedge yourself in case an interview is canceled. However, don't book too many interviews on the same day. Some may run 2 to 3 hours and you may be late getting to the next one. Never be late for an interview! Leave early and allow for bad weather or traffic jams. The single most important thing to remember about the interview is:

DON'T BE NERVOUS !!!

An interview is not a life or death situation. Relax and just be yourself. Easier said than done? Remember that you're not the only person who will be interviewed for the job. They may be interviewing other candidates who come across more relaxed and confident, but don't have the skills and experience you have. Don't let them get the job!

Any decent interviewer understands that you may be nervous, especially if it's one of your very first interviews. He or she should know how to put you at ease right from the start with some light conversation, rather than put you on the spot, but don't count on it. Some interviewers actually enjoy intimidating candidates with out-of-this-world questions or hypothetical situations to see how you react under pressure. Just keep in mind that it's all a show to see what you're made of. Retain your composure as much as possible, thoughtfully consider your replies and maintain eye contact with the interviewer when responding. I recommend reading Martin Yate's *Knock 'Em Dead With Great Answers To Tough Interview Questions* and of course *Getting Hired In The '90s* before any interviewing whatsoever.

No matter how intimidating an interviewer may seem, remember that he or she probably sat right where you are and answered the same questions to get their job. After interviewing hundreds of job applicants, I found the more relaxed the candidate became, the more relaxed I also became. I still asked the tough questions I always did, but our conversation was much more informative and natural.

Get excited about the interview as a discovery process. Be conscientious about talking too much or too little, but feel free to ask questions about the company without appearing skeptical. Try to give the interviewer an honest impression of confidence (without being cocky), personality (don't be a clown) and intelligence (never talk down to the interviewer).

If you are consistently calm and measured in your answers and the interviewer seems inattentive, overbearing, or gives vague responses to questions about compensation, work hours, or specific job duties, don't waste your time. Forget the company and find a better place to spend 40-50 hours of your life every week. Throughout your job search, no matter how hard it seems, you must ALWAYS:

Keep a Positive Attitude; Act Professional and Courteous, with the Receptionist, Everyone.

Dress Like a Professional - Look The Part

The single most important item, as with anything in life, is to keep a positive attitude. Maintain eye contact and speak clearly--on the phone, at the interview, with the receptionist, with everyone. Remember, these people may soon be your co-workers. Everyone wants to be around a winner: act like a winner. **NOW GO GET 'EM !!!**

RESUME INDEX BY PROFESSION:

A

Accounting
  also see Controller
57, 93, 174

Administrative Support: Secretarial, Reception and Customer Service

Architect, Artist
68, 141

Advertising
99

Appraiser: Real Estate
132

Art Gallery Rep.
105

Attorney
  also see Paralegal
61

B

Banking
  see Finance/Banking

C

Chef/Cook
80

Chemistry
  also see Engineering
154

Claims Adjuster
  also see Insurance
145

Communications
  also see Public Relations
157

Computer Sciences, Programming, Analysis Software & Systems, Service, Technical Repair
65, 94, 121, 140

Counseling/Social Services
84, 110

Construction and/or Building Management
103

Controller/Corp. Mgr.
  also see Accounting
108

Credit/Collections
112

Customer Service, Secretary/Receptionist
183, 92

D

Distribution, Freight Routing, Import/Export, Warehousing:
  see Warehousing & Transportation

E

Engineering & Sciences: Nuclear, Petrochemical, Chemical, Genetic, Electrical, Mechanical & Quality CAD/CAM & Design, Management
66, 113, 115, 120, 146, 154, 156, 158, 169

Executive
  also see Management, Sales/Management & Engineering categories
160, 164, 184

F

Facility Management
85

Finance, Banking & Financial Sales
60, 118, 125, 184

Flight Attendant
142

Floral Designer
155

Food Service and Hotel, Hospitality,
  also see Chef/Cook and Restaurant Management
89, 128, 168

G

General Employment
  also see Graduates, new
91, 78, 81, 110, 157

Graduates, new
  also see General Employment
57, 91, 152, 169

H

Hospitality Industries
  see Food Service

Human Resources
54, 166

HVAC Repair/Maintenance
98

I

Insurance/Risk/Underwriter Claims Adjuster
130, 145

L

Loan Officer
  also see Finance/Banking
125

M

Machinist
  also see Tool & Die
109

Military: see Veterans

Management: General
Business, Sales, Product
Lines & Projects
 also see Trainer
58, 74, 158, 164

Manufacturing/Production
133

Marketing
 also see Sales &
Management
99, 74, 180

Mechanics/Power Plant
 Maintenance
95, 116

Mortgage Banking
 also see Finance/Banking
118

N
Nursing/RN
71, 82, 97

O
Office Management
52

P
Paralegal,
Legal Secretary
75, 148

Personnel, Psychology
 see Human Resources &
 Counseling

Pharmaceutical/Medical
Supply Sales;
 also see Sales
111

Pilot/Aircraft Mechanic
 Aviation
116, 127

Plant Manager
 also see Manufacturing &
 Production
133

Police/Law Enforcement
127, 143

Printing
117

Programming & Systems
 see Computer Sciences

Property Management
87

Project Manager
 also see Management,
Plant Mgmt. & Production
182

Psychology
 see Human Resources

Public Relations, Meeting
Planner
72, 157, 149

Purchasing
 also see Management
137,

Q
Quality Assurance
Engineering
 also see Engineering
113,

R
Radiology
139

Real Estate Sales/Leasing
and Management also see
Appraiser
185

Restaurant Management
 also see Food Service
128

Retail Sales/Management
53, 177

S
Sales and
Sales/Management
51, 63, 76, 88, 92, 111,
153, 164, 175, 178

Secretary
92

Social Services: also see
 Counseling

T
Teacher
56, 163

Telecommunications/
Analyst
101, 182

Tool & Die/Shop Machinist
 Operations/Management
69

Trainer
151

Transportation/Railroad,
 Freight Forwarding
 Traffic Management
124, 127, 135, 171, 173

Travel Agent
107

U
Underwriter: see Insurance

V
Veterans/Military
84, 95, 127, 176

W
Warehousing
 also see Transportation
171

Waste Management
 also see Engineering
120

Writer/Creative Fields
 Technical Writing
68, 122

What People Are Saying About

Top Secret Resumes For The '90s!

"Top Secret Resumes For The '90s! gives the reader a wealth of information on how to write an up-to-date resume for today's tough job market...provides sample after sample of well written resumes!"
    Vicki Spina, Author of **Getting Hired In The '90s,** and owner of Corporate Image Publishers/Consultants

"Not just another rehash of the same old formats. Gives explanations of writing and persuasion techniques. The resume and letter samples are excellent..."
    Stephen Pollan, author of books on Personal Finance and the Recession, and commentator on Cable T.V. programs such as Steals & Deals, The Money Wheel and The Answer Man

"Helps take the mystery out of effective resume writing for today's competitive marketplace..."
    Lawrence J. Gorey, President, LJG International, Human Resource Consultant and former Vice President, Personnel and Labor Relations, Coca-Cola Bottling Company of Chicago

"Contains excellent examples, with the right advice for today's job seeker..."
    Paul Silverman, President, The Marshall Group, Executive Search Consultants

"One of the best books I've seen on the subject. Top Secret Resumes For The '90s! is a must for college grads, professionals and executives..."
    Jim Salerno, President, Job Search Techniques, Inc., Career Transition Centers

"Top Secret Resumes For The '90s! is packed with excellent tips and examples...Mr. Provenzano has helped many of our clients with these professional writing techniques..."
    Bill "Buzz" Murphy, President, The Murphy Group, largest employment network in the Chicago area

Douglas County
High School Library
333.1 PRO